SEWING BASKET FUN ™

Edited by Barbara Weiland

HOUSE of
WHITE
BIRCHES
PUBLISHERS
SINCE 1947

Sewing Basket Fun™

Copyright © 2005 House of White Birches, Berne, Indiana 46711

EDITOR	Barbara Weiland
ART DIRECTOR	Brad Snow
PUBLISHING SERVICES MANAGER	Brenda Gallmeyer
MANAGING EDITOR	Barb Sprunger
ASSISTANT ART DIRECTOR	Nick Pierce
COPY SUPERVISOR	Michelle Beck
COPY EDITORS	Conor Allen, Nicki Lehman, Beverly Richardson
TECHNICAL EDITOR	Barbara Weiland
GRAPHIC ARTS SUPERVISOR	Ronda Bechinski
GRAPHIC ARTISTS	Vicki Staggs, Jessi Butler
PRODUCTION ASSISTANTS	Cherly Kempf, Marj Morgan
TECHNICAL ARTISTS	Marla Freeman, Liz Morgan, Jeannette Schilling
PHOTOGRAPHY	Tammy Christian, Christena Green, Carl Clark, Matthew Owen, Nancy Sharp
PHOTO STYLIST	Tammy Nussbaum, Tammy Smith
CHIEF EXECUTIVE OFFICER	John Robinson
PUBLISHING DIRECTOR	David J. McKee
BOOK MARKETING DIRECTOR	Craig Scott
EDITORIAL DIRECTOR	Vivian Rothe
PUBLISHING SERVICES DIRECTOR	Brenda R. Wendling

Printed in China
First Printing: 2005
Library of Congress Control Number: 2004117172
Hardcover ISBN: 1-59217-078-1
Softcover ISBN: 1-59217-090-0

Welcome!

I am so excited to present these beautiful and fun-to-sew projects created by so many talented designers for your sewing enjoyment. It's been lots of fun to choose the items for this book and prepare them for you. Whenever you feel the urge to open your sewing basket and turn on your sewing machine, you're sure to find just the project to sew for yourself or to give as gift.

Sewing Basket Fun is divided into four sections—one for each season of the year. Each one features projects in colors and themes that reflect the changes we witness in nature throughout the year. There are plenty of items that are easy to sew and won't take too long to complete. Stitch up a welcome banner, sew something wonderful to wear, or make a cozy lap quilt. Home dec accessories to freshen your seasonal decor and fun handbags are also included. Of course for winter, there are several home decor items to help you decorate for the season, including stockings, festive pillows and winter-warming pieces made from comfy-cozy fleece.

Most projects also include extra tips for sewing success, and some include ideas for choosing different fabrics and colors to quick-change it to another season. I hope you'll take a few minutes right now to peruse the pages and mark the projects you want to make right away. Then head to your sewing room, turn on your favorite music and get started. If you're like me, you probably already have the makings for some of these things in your sewing room stash or scrap basket.

Have fun using the tools in your sewing basket to stitch up the seasons in style!

Barbara

Barbara Weiland

Contents

Spring Sparklers

Summer Sizzlers

Autumn Accents

Winter Wonders

Spring Sparklers

Here's a garden full of projects that sparkle with springtime appeal and glisten like raindrops on the season's colorful flowers.

Floral Basket Bouquet

Use this pretty metal basket filled with seasonal silk flowers and embellished with a colorful quilt square as a substitute for a door wreath come spring. Adjust the colors for the patchwork and flowers to suit your spring decorating theme, or gear it to other seasons or holidays with suitable color choices.

DESIGN BY DENISE CLASON

Project Specifications
Basket: Approximately 12 x 12 x 4 inches, excluding flowers

Materials
- 7-inch square of lavender tone-on-tone print for block center
- 6-inch square of yellow tone-on-tone print for flower appliqué
- ⅛ yard green floral print for block corners
- ⅛ yard peach tone-on-tone print for block triangles and flower center
- Scrap of green print for leaves
- 6-inch square of fusible interfacing
- Pencil
- 8-inch square of iron-on, tear-away stabilizer
- 10-inch square of muslin
- 10-inch square of cotton batting
- ¼ yard lightweight paper-backed fusible web
- All-purpose sewing thread to match fabrics
- Rotary cutter, mat and ruler

Basket Supplies
- 12 x 12 x 4-inch metal basket with handle
- 1-inch-wide wash brush
- Olive-yellow and white acrylic paint
- Matte varnish
- Craft glue appropriate for metal and fabric
- Hold the Foam! glue from Beacon Adhesives
- Silk flowers
    - 2 sprays of dark purple roses
    - 2 sprays of rose leaves
    - 3 sprays of pink/mauve filler flowers
    - 1 spray of sunflowers
- 2 x 12 x 18-inch block of green florist foam
- 2-inch-wide wire-edged ribbon to complement floral arrangement
- Seam sealant
- Spray starch
- Craft stick for spreading glue
- 100-grit sanding disc
- Green floral tape

Instructions

Project Note: *All seam allowances are ¼ inch wide.*

Step 1. Cut one 6⅞-inch square from lavender tone-on-tone print. Cut four 2¾-inch squares from the green floral print. Cut four 3⅛-inch squares from the peach print. Cut once diagonally for eight half-square triangles.

Step 2. Sew two peach triangles to adjacent edges of each green square. Press the seams toward the triangles.

Step 3. Mark the center of each side of the lavender square and the center of the long edge of each pieced triangle unit from Step 2. Matching centers, sew a unit from Step 3 to opposite sides of the square and press the seams toward the square (Fig. 1).

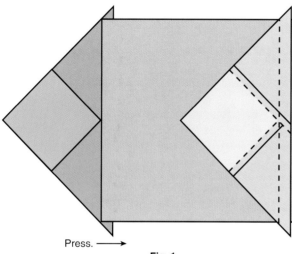

Press. ⟶

Fig. 1
Sew pieced units to opposite
sides of center square.

Step 4. Repeat with the remaining triangle units to complete the block (Fig. 2).

Step 5. Apply the 6-inch square of fusible interfacing to the wrong side of the 6-inch yellow tone-on-tone print square following manufacturer's directions.

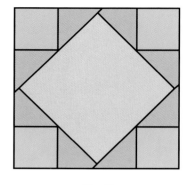

Fig. 2
Pieced Block.

Step 6. Using the templates on page 11, trace the flower, flower center and two leaves onto the paper side of the fusible web. Cut out each piece, leaving a ¼-inch-wide margin beyond the drawn lines. Position on the wrong side of the appropriate fabrics and cut out on the lines.

Step 7. Center the flower on the quilt block and the flower center and leaves. Fuse in place following the manufacturer's directions. Apply a piece of iron-on, tear-away stabilizer to the wrong side of the block.

Step 8. Adjust the machine for 2.5mm-wide satin stitch. Using thread to match each piece, satin-stitch each one in place. Remove the stabilizer and press the block adding spray starch for a nice finish.

Step 9. Place the block face up on the batting and backing and pin the layers together. Machine-baste ⅛ inch from the outer edges. Stitch in the ditch of the seam around the center square (Fig. 3). Add more quilting as desired.

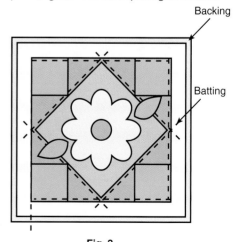

Backing

Batting

Fig. 3
Stitch in the ditch
around center square.

Make It Yours

The colors for this basket of flowers can be changed to your color palette. Add some pinks, yellows and greens or try using Christmas colors with red, green and gold for the holiday season. Instead of the spring flowers, add some holiday greenery and silk poinsettias. Or, consider using some rust, gold, olive and brown fabrics for the quilt block and fall colors for the silk flowers. Add oak and maple leaves as an accent.

If you apply self-adhesive hook-and-loop tape to the quilt-block perimeter and to the metal basket, you can interchange blocks for each season or holiday you are celebrating.

Step 10. Trim the quilted block if necessary to "square it up."

Step 11. Sand the metal basket with a 100-grit sanding disc. Wipe off the dust with an old rag.

Step 12. With the 1-inch wash brush, paint basket with olive-yellow paint and allow to dry. Add a second coat of paint and allow to dry.

Step 13. Using a clean 1-inch wash brush, dry-brush white paint in a crisscrossing pattern over the green. Allow to dry thoroughly.

Note: Dry brushing is a technique that gives a soft look to a painted piece. Dip the brush into the white paint, and then brush the excess onto a paper towel so the bristles are "dry." Most of the paint should be gone so that only a touch of paint is left to cover the olive-green coat.

Step 14. With a clean 1-inch wash brush, finish the basket with a coat of matte varnish and allow to dry.

Step 15. Glue the quilt block to the front of the metal basket using glue appropriate for metal and fabric. Use a wooden craft stick to spread the glue on the back of the block and center the block on the basket front. Allow to dry in a well-ventilated area.

Step 16. Cut the foam block into a shape that will fit snugly inside the basket and glue in place.

Step 17. Adjust the length of the silk flower stems as needed so that you can create a pleasing floral arrangement in the basket. Use the rose leaves as the background layer, cutting sprays apart if necessary for easier arranging. If you need to lengthen wires after cutting stems apart, add wire and wrap with green floral tape. After placing the leaves, arrange the remaining silk flowers in your hand or lay them down on a table to get the look you want. Insert into the foam and adjust as needed.

Step 18. Use the wire-edged ribbon to make a bow around the handle and shape it as desired. Cut the ribbon ends on a slight angle and apply a seam sealant to prevent the ends from fraying. ❖

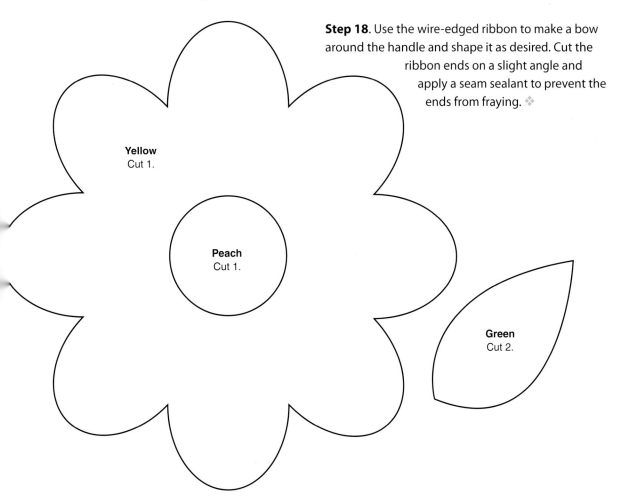

Yellow
Cut 1.

Peach
Cut 1.

Green
Cut 2.

Flower Basket Bouquet Templates
Actual Size

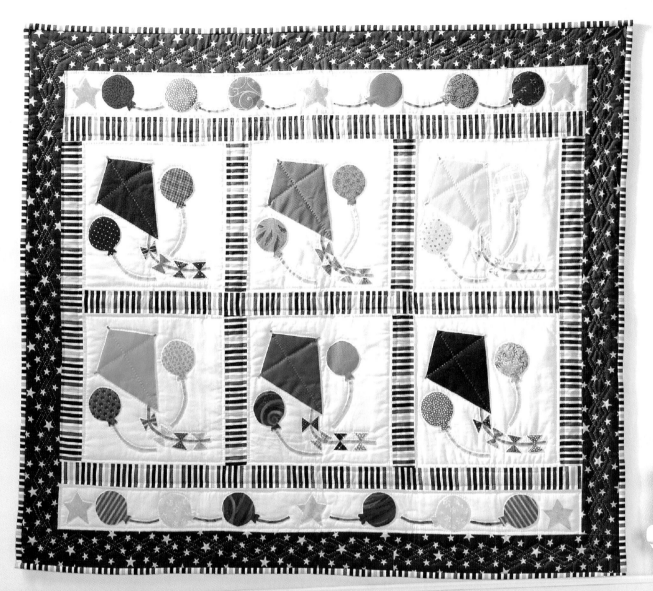

Go Fly a Kite
Wall Quilt

Bright balloons and colorful kites sail across a clear sky in this cheerful wall quilt. Primary colors are the perfect accent for a baby's or toddler's room. Fast-fused appliqué makes this a quick project to sew in a weekend.

DESIGN BY EILEEN WESTFALL

Project Specifications

Quilt Size: 42 x 36½ inches

Materials

- ⅞ yards 44/45-inch-wide white solid or tone-on-tone print
- ¾ yard 44/45-inch-wide multicolored striped print
- ½ yard 44/45-inch-wide red print for the borders
- 6 x 7-inch piece of solid-color fabric for the kites in each of the following colors: red, orange, yellow, green, blue and purple
- Assorted scraps of gray, brown, red, orange, yellow, green, blue and purple prints for the balloons, kite tails and the strings
- 1¼ yards 44/45-inch-wide blue print for the backing
- 1 yard paper-backed fusible web
- 44 x 39-inch piece of batting
- All-purpose thread to match fabrics
- Pencil
- Rotary cutter, mat and ruler
- Press cloth
- Basic sewing tools and equipment

Instructions

Project Notes: *Preshrink all fabrics and press to remove wrinkles. Cutting is based on a usable width of 43 inches after preshrinking. If fabric is narrower, you may need additional yardage. All seam allowances are ¼ inch wide. Press all seams toward the striped sashing strips with the exception of the outer border seams. Refer to Fig. 1 for all assembly steps.*

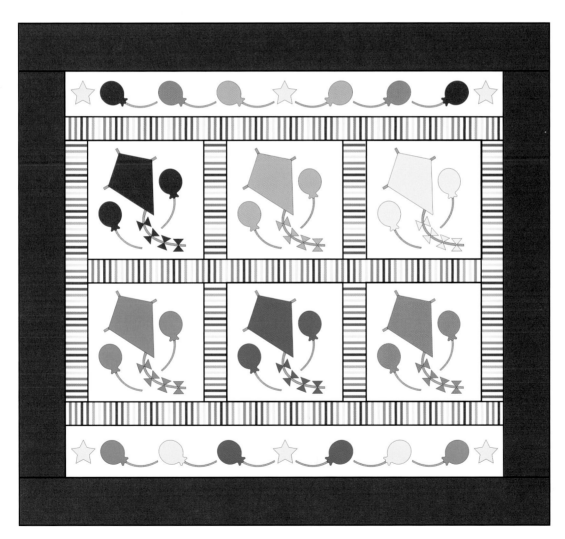

Fig. 1
Quilt Assembly

Step 1. From the white fabric, cut six 10½-inch squares for the blocks and two strips each 3½ x 36½ inches for the appliquéd top and bottom borders. From the multicolored stripe, cut four strips each 2 x 10½ inches for the vertical sashing, one strip 2 x 33½ inches for the horizontal sashing between the block rows, two strips each 2 x 22 inches for the side sashing and two strips each 2½ x 36½ inches for the top and bottom sashing. For double-layer, ⅜-inch-wide finished binding, cut four strips each 2½ x 43 inches. From the red print, cut two strips each 3½ x 31 inches and two strips each 3½ x 42½ inches for the borders. From the blue print, cut one piece 44 x 39 inches for the backing.

Step 2. Using the templates on page 15 and leaving a ¼-inch-wide margin between motifs, trace the required number of each onto the paper side of fusible web. Cut out each shape with a ⅛-inch margin beyond the drawn lines. Position each appliqué on the wrong side of the required fabric color and fuse in place following the manufacturer's directions. Cut out on the drawn lines. ***Note:*** *If you prefer, eliminate the kite and balloon string appliqués and embroider them instead using three strands of embroidery floss (gray for balloons and brown for the kite tails). Use a chain stitch or the stem stitch.*

Step 3. Sew the white squares together in two rows of three squares each with 2 x 10½-inch striped sashing strips between them; press. Sew the two rows together with a 2 x 33½-inch striped sashing strip between them; press.

Step 4. Sew the 2 x 22-inch striped sashing strips to the short sides of the quilt top and press. Add the remaining 2 x 36½ sashing strips to the top and bottom edges. Press.

Step 5. Sew a 3½ x 36½-inch white strip to the upper and lower edges of the pieced center. Sew the 3½ x 31-inch red border strips to opposite sides of the quilt top and press the seams toward the borders. Add the 3½ x 42½-inch red borders to the top and bottom edges to complete the pieced top. Press.

Step 6. Remove the backing paper from each appliqué and position them on the quilt blocks in numerical order. Use pins to hold temporarily. When satisfied with the arrangement, use the tip of the iron to fuse-baste the appliqués in place. Remove the pins and place a press cloth on top of the fuse-basted appliqués. Fuse in place following the manufacturer's directions. Position and appliqué balloons and stars to the white strips in the same manner.

Step 7. Layer the quilt top with batting and backing and smooth out any wrinkles. Baste the layers together. Quilt as desired. Trim the excess batting and backing even with the quilt-top edges.

Step 8. Measure the quilt-top length through the center of the quilt and trim two of the 2½-inch-wide striped binding strips this length. Sew to the top and bottom edges of the quilt top using a ⅜-inch-wide seam.

Step 9. Measure the quilt width through the center and add ¾ inch. Trim the remaining binding strips to this length and use to bind the top and bottom edges of the quilt, turning in the raw edges at each end for a neat finish. ❖

Freezer-Paper Appliqué

This quilt features fused appliqué. If you prefer to do hand appliqué, cut each shape from freezer paper and apply the waxed side of the paper to the wrong side of the fabric scrap with a dry iron. Add a ¼-inch-wide allowance around each appliqué shape when you cut it out. Turn the allowance snugly over the edge of each freezer-paper shape and hand-baste in place to prepare the appliqués (Fig. 2). To remove the paper, make a small cut in the fabric behind the appliqué and carefully pull the paper out with your fingers or scissors.

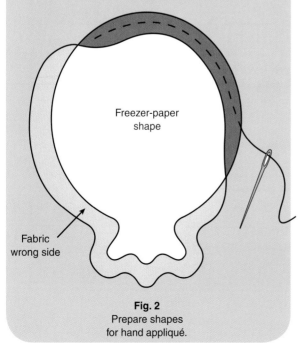

Freezer-paper shape

Fabric wrong side

Fig. 2
Prepare shapes
for hand appliqué.

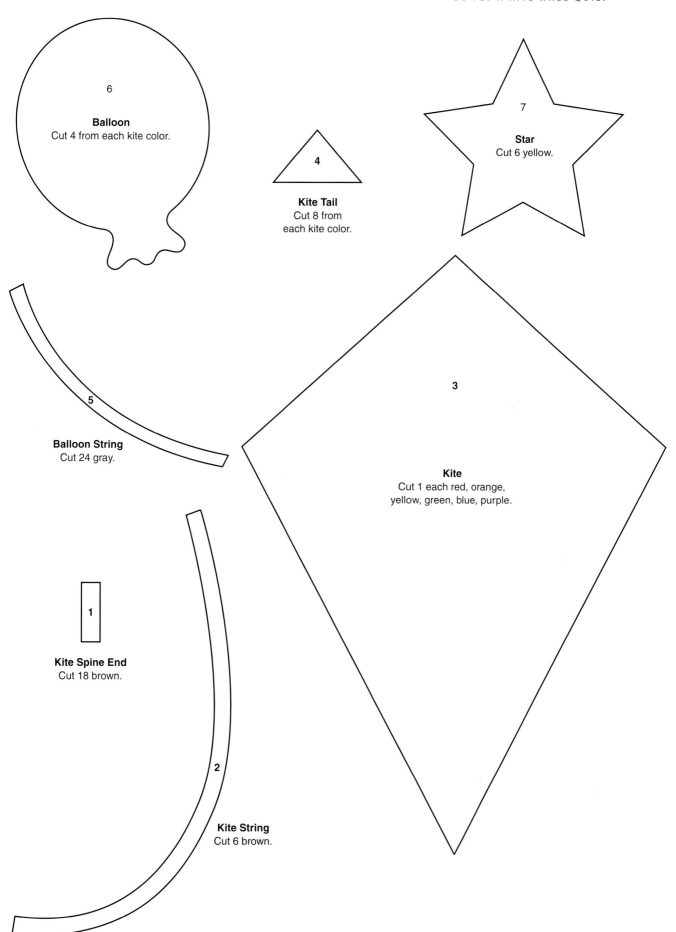

6

Balloon
Cut 4 from each kite color.

4

Kite Tail
Cut 8 from
each kite color.

7

Star
Cut 6 yellow.

5

Balloon String
Cut 24 gray.

3

Kite
Cut 1 each red, orange,
yellow, green, blue, purple.

1

Kite Spine End
Cut 18 brown.

2

Kite String
Cut 6 brown.

Butterbees & Bumbleflies Kitchen Ensemble

These "buzzy" cook's accessories in bright springtime colors are easy to sew and fun to use. They make great gifts to stitch up in a hurry.

DESIGNS BY PAM LINDQUIST

Project Specifications

Bumblefly Apron: 26 x 32 inches, excluding ties
Bumblefly Potholder: 9 x 10½ inches
Butterbee Potholder: 9½ x 11 inches
Butterbee Kitchen Towel: 17 x 27 inches

Materials
Bumblefly Apron
- 1½ yards 44/45-inch-wide green daisy print
- 7 x 8-inch rectangle yellow print
- 2½ x 4-inch rectangle black-and-white check
- 12-inch square black fabric for body outline
- 12-inch square red fabric for wing outline
- 7 x 11-inch rectangle paper-backed fusible web
- Tailor's chalk

Bumblefly Potholder
- 11 x 12-inch rectangle black-and-yellow checked print
- 11 x 22-inch rectangle yellow print
- 11 x 12-inch rectangle yellow backing fabric
- 12-inch square red fabric
- 11 x 12-inch rectangle Insul-Bright/Mylar batting or Teflon-coated fabric
- 11 x 12-inch rectangle cotton batting

Butterbee Potholder
- 9 x 12-inch rectangle black fabric
- 12 x 14-inch rectangle yellow fabric
- 9 x 18-inch rectangle white fabric
- 12-inch square yellow floral print for binding
- 11 x 12-inch rectangle Insul-Bright/Mylar batting or Teflon-coated fabric
- 11 x 12-inch rectangle cotton batting

Butterbee Kitchen Towel
- 17 x 27-inch yellow kitchen towel
- 4 x 19-inch strip yellow-and-white checked print
- 3 x 8-inch strip black-and-yellow striped print for the bodies
- 3 x 14-inch strip black-and-white print for the wings
- 5 (¾-inch-diameter) black buttons
- 24 inches black embroidery floss
- 9 x 12-inch rectangle paper-backed fusible web
- 1 package ready-made black piping
- 1 package white jumbo rickrack

All Projects
- All-purpose thread to match fabrics
- Rotary cutter, mat and ruler
- Basic sewing tools and equipment

Instructions
Bumblefly Apron

Project Notes: *This apron is designed to fit an average-size woman (12-14-16). Adjust as needed for a larger or smaller apron. Ten inches is average for the measurement from the top of the apron to the waistline. Make the apron wider for larger sizes by adding to the side edges. Be sure to calculate the yardage for a different size before buzzing off to your favorite fabric store. All measurements include ¼-inch-wide seam allowances unless otherwise stated.*

Step 1. From the green daisy print, cut one rectangle 27 x 35½ inches, one rectangle 9½ x 19½ inches and four strips each 2½ x 42 inches. From the black fabric square, cut one bias strip 1 x 15 inches. From the red fabric square, cut two bias strips each 1 x 15 inches.

Step 2. Use the templates on page 22 for the bumblefly. Cut one body and one complete wing piece from the appropriate fabrics.

Step 3. Refer to Fig. 1 for Steps 1–5. Make a ¼-inch-wide double hem at the side edges of the 27 x 35½-inch apron panel. At the upper edge, turn under and press ¼-inch, then turn under an additional 1 inch and stitch in place. Hem the lower edge in the same manner but use a total hem allowance of 2¼ inches.

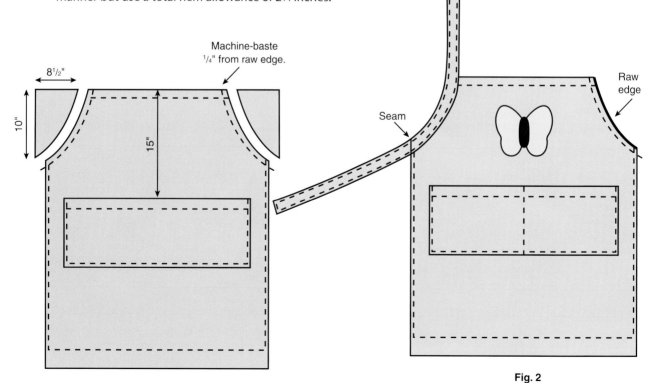

Fig. 1
Apron Assembly

Fig. 2
Slip folded edges of apron tie over armhole edge stitches.

Step 4. To shape the armholes, mark and cut away a section at each side edge as shown in Fig. 1. Cut the first one and use it as a pattern to cut the second armhole. Machine-baste ¼ inch from each armhole edge.

Step 5. For the pocket, turn under and press ¼ inch at the short edges of the 9½ x 19½-inch rectangle. Repeat at the top and bottom edges. At the upper edge, turn under an additional 1 inch and press. Stitch in place.

Step 6. Position the apron pocket 15 inches from the apron upper edge and centered between both side edges. Pin and stitch in place along the side and bottom edges.

Step 7. Use chalk to draw a dividing line through the center of the pocket. Pin in place and stitch on the chalk line, backstitching at the top and bottom edges of the pocket.

Step 8. Sew the 2½-inch-wide strips together in pairs to make two long strips. Turn under and press ¼ inch at each short end of each strip. Repeat along both long edges. Fold the strips in half with wrong sides together and turned edges even. Press.

Step 9. With the seam in the strip at the lower edge of the armhole, slip the folded edges of each strip over an armhole edge. Pin in place with the folded edges along the basting. Pin the folded edges together above and below the armhole edges. Stitch ⅛ inch from the folded edges to complete the ties (Fig. 2 at left).

Step 10. Prepare the bumblefly appliqués for your favorite method: hand, machine or fusible. Center the bumblefly wings approximately 2 inches below the apron upper edge and appliqué in place using your favorite method. Add the body and appliqué in place.

Step 11. Sew the red bias strips together to make a strip approximately 30 inches long. Fold the strip in half lengthwise with wrong sides together and raw edges even. Stitch ¼ inch from the raw edges and trim the seam allowance to ⅛ inch. With the seam centered in the tube, press the seam allowance to one side.

Step 12. With the seam side down, shape the bias tube around the outer edges of the wings. Hand- or machine-stitch in place along both folded edges.

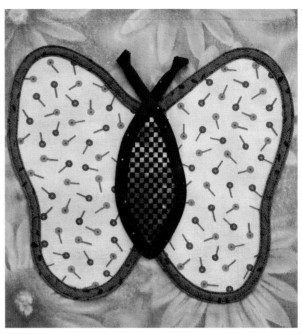

Prepare a black bias tube in the same manner and use it to outline the body, allowing 2 inches of bias for the antennae. Tie an overhand knot at the end of each antenna and trim any excess.

Bumblefly Potholder

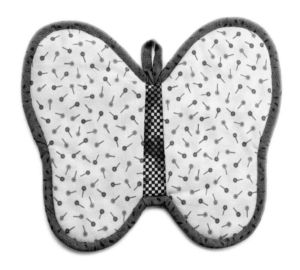

Project Note: *All measurements include ½-inch-wide seam allowances unless otherwise noted.*

Step 1. Make patterns for the bumblefly body and wing shapes using the templates on page 23. Cut the bumblefly body and wings from the fabrics indicated.

Step 2. Cut out three 2 x 15-inch bias strips from the red fabric. Sew the strips together with bias seams to make one long strip.

Step 3. Place the 11 x 12-inch rectangle of yellow backing fabric wrong side up, and then add the Insul-Bright followed by the cotton batting. Center the bumblefly body right side up on top of the batting.

Step 4. Fold a wing in half wrong sides together and position it on top of the body with raw edges even. Repeat with the remaining wing. Pin all layers together.

Step 5. Machine-baste ¼ inch from the raw edge of the bumblefly. Trim the excess layers even with the bumblefly body edges.

Step 6. Turn under and press a scant ½ inch along one long edge of the red bias strip. Turn under and press ¼ inch at one diagonal end of the bias. With right sides together and raw edges even, pin the bias to the outer edge of the potholder. Begin at one side of the shape and when you reach the head allow a 3-inch length for the loop before continuing to pin the bias in place. When you reach the folded end at the beginning, trim the excess bias allowing a ½- to 1-inch overlap. Trim the excess binding.

Step 7. Sew the binding to the potholder using a scant ½-inch-wide seam allowance. Remove the pins.

Step 8. Fold the bias over the raw edges to the back of the potholder and sew in place by hand. When turning the bias to the back at the excess left for the hanging loop, the binding will form a tuck at the corner where the head and wing join. Hand-sew in place. Hand-sew the loop edges together, tucking in the raw edges of the bias binding before continuing to sew the remainder of the bias binding to the back of the potholder (Fig. 3).

Fig. 3
Make loop and hand-sew
tucks and folded edges together.

Butterbee Potholder

Project Note: *All measurements include a ½-inch-wide seam allowance unless otherwise noted.*

Step 1. From the yellow fabric, cut two strips each 1½ x 12 inches and one rectangle 11 x 12 inches. From the black fabric scraps, cut one strip 2 x 12 inches, one strip, 3 x 12 inches and one strip 4 x 12 inches. From the white fabric, cut two squares each 9 x 9 inches. From the yellow floral print, cut three bias strips each 2 x 15 inches.

Step 2. Alternate the black and yellow fabric strips to make the body and sew together using ¼-inch-wide seams. Press the seams in one direction. Using the

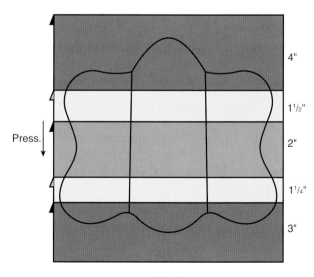

Fig. 4
Cut butterbee from
pieced panel.

templates on page 23, cut the wings from the fabric as directed on the template. Center the body on the pieced fabric panel, pin in place and cut out (Fig. 4).

Step 3. With the 11 x 12-inch rectangle of yellow fabric wrong side up, add the 11 x 12-inch rectangle of Insul-Bright followed by the 11 x 12-inch rectangle of batting. Center the butterbee body on top, right side up.

Step 4. Fold a wing in half with wrong sides together and position on top of the body with raw edges even. Repeat with the remaining wing. Pin all layers together (Fig. 5). Machine-baste ¼ inch from the butterbee raw edges and trim the excess batting and backing layers even with the raw edges.

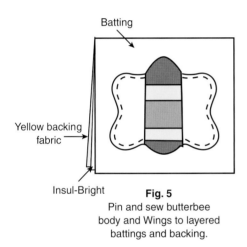

Fig. 5
Pin and sew butterbee body and Wings to layered battings and backing.

Step 5. Turn under and press a scant ½ inch along one long edge of the yellow print binding strip. Follow Steps 4–6 of the directions for the Bumblefly Potholder to complete the potholder with a hanging loop.

Butterbee Kitchen Towel

Step 1. Choose your favorite appliqué method: hand, machine or fusible. Using the templates on page 23, cut the required pieces from the appropriate fabrics as directed.

Step 2. Beginning at the center of the yellow-and-white checked strip, position the wings for the first butterbee with the upper edges of the wings 1¾ inches from the upper raw edge of the strip. Appliqué in place. Add the remaining wings, spacing them about 1 inch apart. Appliqué a body in the center of each set of wings.

Step 3. Using black thread in the sewing machine needle, satin-stitch around the outer edges of the butterbee bodies and wings.

Step 4. Using 3 strands of black embroidery floss, embroider the antennae with a simple stem or running stitch. Add a French knot at the end of each antenna.

Step 5. Sew a black button in place for each bee's head.

Step 6. With right sides together and raw edges even, machine-baste black piping to each long edge of the yellow-and-white strip.

Step 7. Position a piece of jumbo rickrack on top of each piped edge with the outer point of the rickrack at the raw edge of the piping. Pin in place. Use ¼-inch-wide seam allowance to baste the rickrack in place.

Step 8. Turn the rickrack and piping seam allowance to the wrong side of the band and press.

Step 9. Position the band 3 inches above the lower edge of the towel, making sure the middle bee is centered along the towel width. Pin the band in place and trim excess at each edge, leaving a ½-inch-wide turn-under allowance. Turn the raw edges under even with the finished edges of the towel. Press. Slipstitch to the towel edge.

Step 10. Attach the zipper foot and stitch the band to the towel, positioning the foot and needle to stitch in the ditch of the piping seam. ❖

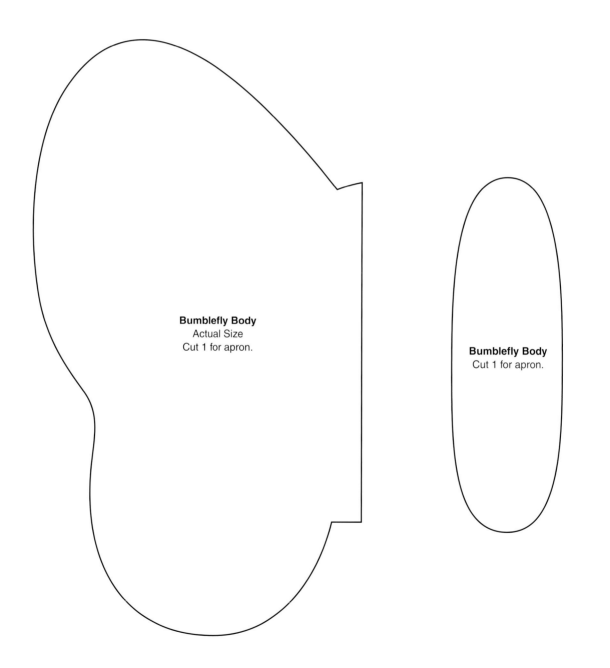

Bumblefly Body
Actual Size
Cut 1 for apron.

Bumblefly Body
Cut 1 for apron.

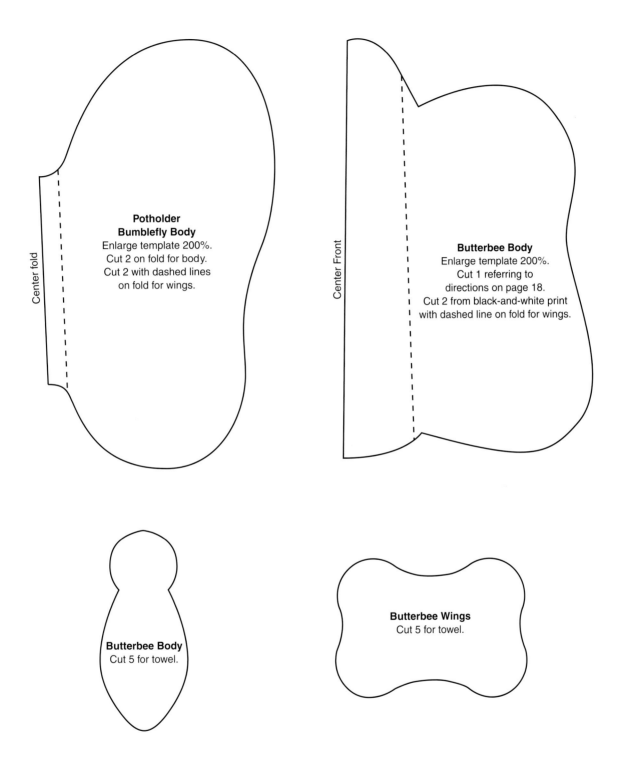

Center fold

Potholder
Bumblefly Body
Enlarge template 200%.
Cut 2 on fold for body.
Cut 2 with dashed lines
on fold for wings.

Center Front

Butterbee Body
Enlarge template 200%.
Cut 1 referring to
directions on page 18.
Cut 2 from black-and-white print
with dashed line on fold for wings.

Butterbee Body
Cut 5 for towel.

Butterbee Wings
Cut 5 for towel.

Stripe It Rich Pillow Duo

Make these two decorator pillows to discover the fun of working with stripes. It's easy to achieve two different looks with the same fabric by creating mitered designs.

DESIGNS BY CAROL ZENTGRAF

Project Specifications

Stripes Go Square Pillow: 14 inches square, excluding trim

All Points to Center Pillow: 18 inches square, excluding trim

Materials
Stripes Go Square Pillow

- 1 yard 54-inch-wide striped decorator fabric
- 1⅝ yards sew-in brush fringe
- 14-inch square pillow form
- Repositionable ½-inch-wide fusible web
- Permanent fabric adhesive
- Pattern tracing cloth or pattern paper
- All-purpose thread to match fabrics
- Rotary cutter, mat and ruler
- Basic sewing tools and equipment

All Points to Center Pillow

- 1⅓ yards 54-inch-wide striped decorator fabric
- 2⅛ yards tassel fringe with decorative header
- 18-inch-square pillow form
- Pattern tracing cloth or pattern paper
- All-purpose thread to match fabrics
- Repositionable ½-inch-wide fusible web
- Permanent fabric adhesive
- Rotary cutter, mat and ruler
- Basic sewing tools and equipment

Stripes Go Square Pillow

Project Note: *All seam allowances are ½ inch wide.*

Step 1. Draw a 15-inch square on pattern tracing cloth or paper. Divide the square in half twice diagonally. Add ½-inch-wide seam allowances to all edges of one of the triangles. Cut out the triangle with the seam allowances to use for your pattern (Fig. 1).

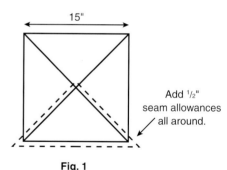

15"

Add ¹/₂"
seam allowances
all around.

Fig. 1
Make paper pattern for triangle.

Step 2. Place the pattern on the striped fabric with the base of the triangle parallel to the stripes. Cut the first triangle. Use it as a guide to cut a total of eight identical triangles (four for the front and four for the back).

Step 3. Sew triangles together in pairs to make four identical triangles with perfectly matched stripes (see the sidebar on page 26). Press the seams open.

Step 4. Sew two large triangles together along the long edge to create a square. Use the fusible web method in the side bar to ensure a perfect match (Fig. 2). Repeat for the pillow back.

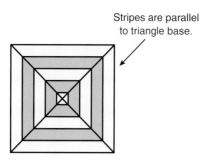

Stripes are parallel to triangle base.

Fig. 2
Sew triangles together.
Make 2.

Step 5. With right sides together, baste the heading of the brush fringe to the outer edge of one pillow square, overlapping the ends neatly. The loops of the fringe should point to the center of the pillow square.

Step 6. With right sides together, sew the pillow back to the pillow front, leaving a 6-inch-long opening in

one side. Clip across the corners and turn the pillow cover right side out. Press, turning under the seam allowances at the opening.

Step 7. Insert the pillow form and slipstitch the opening closed.

All Points to Center Pillow

Project Note: *All seam allowances are ½ inch wide.*

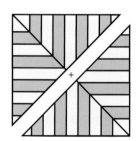

Step 1. Draw a 19-inch square on pattern tracing cloth or paper. Add seam allowances and cut out as directed in Step 1 for the Stripes Go Square Pillow.

Step 2. Place the pattern on the fabric with the triangle base perpendicular to the stripes and cut the first triangle. Use it as a guide to cut a total of eight identical triangles.

Step 3. Sew the triangles together in pairs with stripes matching perfectly (see the sidebar) to make four large triangles. Press the seams open.

Step 4. Sew the resulting triangles together in pairs and press the seams open. Take care to match the stripes at the seam line using the same fusible-tape method (Fig. 3).

Fig. 3
Sew triangle pairs together.

Step 5. Sew the pillow front to the back ½ inch from all edges, leaving a 6-inch-long opening for turning in one side. Clip the seam allowances at each corner and turn the pillow cover right side out. Press, turning under the seam allowances at the opening.

Step 6. Beginning at the center of one edge, use permanent fabric adhesive to glue the trim in place along the pillow edges and create a neatly turned overlap at the point where the ends join.

Step 7. Insert the pillow form and slipstitch the opening closed. ❖

Miter Perfect!

1. To match the stripes perfectly, machine-baste ½ inch from the edge of one triangle. Apply repositionable sticky-back fusible web along the stitching in the seam allowance (Fig. 4).

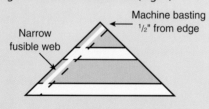

Machine basting ¹/₂" from edge

Narrow fusible web

Fig. 4
Place respositionable fusible web in seam allowance.

2. Position a second triangle face down on the first triangle aligning the edges to be joined. Finger-press the taped edges together. Carefully lift the top fabric layer to make certain the stripes are aligned. Adjust if necessary.

3. When you are sure the layers are positioned for a perfect match, fuse in place following the manufacturer's directions. Stitch ½ inch from the raw edges and remove any basting that shows. Press the seam allowances to one side. *Note: You can adapt this technique, using double-sided basting tape if you prefer not to fuse the seams together.*

Place Mats With Pizzazz

Serve up some springtime sizzle with these bright linen place mats. Make all four the same or mix it up like these festive, color-blocked table toppers. Cue them to your decorating scheme or make a set for each season in appropriate colors.

DESIGN BY PAM ARCHER

Project Specifications
Place Mat Size: 15 x 18 inches

Materials for Four Place Mats
- 1 yard each of four different light- to medium-weight linen fabrics in desired colors (yardage allows for preshrinking)
- 5¼ yards 22-inch-wide, lightweight weft-insertion or woven fusible interfacing
- 4 (14-inch) squares of lightweight, paper-backed fusible web
- ¼ x 6-inch strips of fusible web
- Iron-on, tear-away stabilizer
- Optional: Thin cotton batting and temporary spray adhesive for padded place mats
- All-purpose thread to match fabrics
- Rayon embroidery thread to match fabrics
- Bobbin thread for embroidery
- Open-toe embroidery foot
- ¼-inch presser foot (optional)
- Rotary cutter, mat and ruler
- Basic sewing tools and equipment

Instructions
Project Note: *When assembling the place mats, match the thread color and place mat back to the oval color on the place mat front.*

Step 1. Wash the linen fabrics in hot water to preshrink. You may need to wash them separately to control any bleeding in the wash water. Dry to the just-damp stage and press to remove all wrinkles.

Step 2. From each of the four fabrics, cut one 17 x 20-inch rectangle for the place mat backs and one 14-inch square for the ovals. From each of the four fabrics, cut two pieces each 8½ x 19 inches for the place mat fronts.

Step 3. From the fusible interfacing, cut matching squares and rectangles for each of the linen pieces (a total of 16) cut in Step 2. Cut them ⅛ inch narrower and shorter than the linen pieces.

Make It Yours

Choose colors that coordinate with your dishes when selecting fabrics for these place mats. If you like to do serger projects, this design offers lots of possibilities. Use decorative thread in the loopers for these serger techniques.

• Flatlock the narrow rectangles together with a wide, closely spaced stitch.

• Serge-finish the oval edges with a wide, closely spaced stitch; position the oval on the place mat front and fuse in place. For added security, stitch in place at the outer and inner edges of the serging with matching thread.

• Place the place mat front and back wrong sides together and baste ¼ inch from the raw edges. Trim the back even with the front and then serge-finish the outer edges together, turning neat corners.

Step 4. Apply fusible interfacing to the wrong side of each fabric square and rectangle following the manufacturer's directions.

Step 5. Arrange the narrow rectangles for the place mat fronts in pairs in the desired color combinations.

Step 6. Using a ¼-inch-wide seam and with right sides facing, sew the rectangles together in pairs. (The fusible interfacing will help control raveling in the linen fabric.) Press the seams open.

Step 7. Cut four 4 x 19-inch strips of iron-on, tear-away stabilizer and apply to the wrong side of each place mat front, centering it over the seam.

Step 8. Adjust the machine for a 3.5mm-wide satin stitch. On the right side of each place mat front, satin stitch across the seam for 3½ inches at each end of the seam. Use rayon embroidery thread in the needle to match the oval and backing color for each mat (Fig. 1). Use bobbin thread for embroidery in the bobbin and test the satin stitch on scraps to make sure the bobbin thread doesn't pull up to the right side. Use an open-toe embroidery foot, if available, so you can center the seam under the stitching. Remove the stabilizer.

Step 9. Apply a piece of paper-backed fusible web to the wrong side of each 14-inch square following

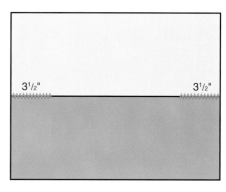

Fig. 1
Satin-stitch for 3½" at
each end of seam with thread to
match oval and backing color.

manufacturer's directions. Referring to Fig. 2, fold a 10 x 13½-inch piece of paper in half twice and draw an oval pattern shape. Cut out the pattern and draw a grainline arrow on the true diagonal so the ovals will be cut on the bias. Use the pattern to draw an oval pattern on the paper side of the fusible web on each square. Cut out each oval.

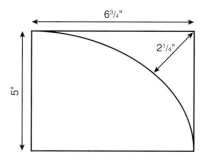

Fig. 2
Make paper pattern for oval.

Step 10. One by one, remove the paper backing from the ovals and center each one on its mat front. Fuse in place following the manufacturer's directions. To aid in placement, fold the oval in half lengthwise with the paper side out and crease it at the short ends. Align the creases with the center seam line.

Step 11. For each place mat, cut a 12 x 15-inch piece of tear-away stabilizer. Center the stabilizer on the wrong side of each mat behind the oval.

Step 12. On the right side, finish the raw edges of each oval with satin stitching to match the stitching along the center seam. Remove the stabilizer.

Step 13. Using rotary-cutting tools, trim each completed place mat front to 15½ x 18½ inches, taking

care to keep the oval centered from side to side and from upper to lower edges.

Step 14. With right sides together, center each place mat front on the 17 x 20-inch back that matches the oval color. Pin around all edges, leaving a 6-inch-long section unpinned in one long edge.

Step 15. Attach the ¼-inch presser foot and stitch ¼ inch from the place mat front edges, beginning and ending with backstitching at the pins that mark the opening (Fig.3). If you don't have a ¼-inch foot, use the edge of a standard presser foot as the guide and adjust the needle position to the right to create a ¼-inch-wide seam—or simply use the edge of the foot

as your guide. If you do, the place mats will be just a bit smaller than the finished dimensions cited above. *Note: When you have stitched to within 1 inch of the corner, stop and shorten the stitch length to 18–20 stitches per inch. Continue stitching but rather than pivoting at the corner, stop shy of the corner and pivot so that there are two or three short stitches across the point. This will allow for more smoothly turned and stronger corners (Fig. 3).*

Step 16. Trim the excess back even with the raw edges of the place mat front. Clip the corners as shown to eliminate bulk (Fig. 4).

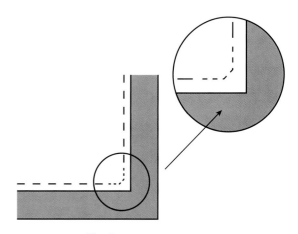

Fig. 4
Use shorter stitches at corner
and across the point.

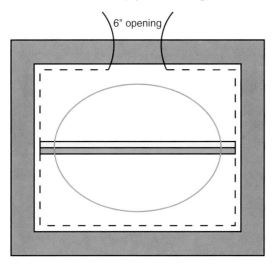

Fig. 3
Stitch place mat front to back
¼" from edges.

6" opening

Step 17. Optional: For padded place mats, cut a 15½ x 18½-inch piece of thin batting for each place mat. Apply a light coat of temporary spray adhesive to one side of the batting. Center and smooth the wrong side of the back of the stitched place mat in place on the batting. Flip the place mat over and stitch again on top of the first stitching. Lift the edge of the batting and trim it close to the stitching.

Step 18. Turn the place mat right side out and press carefully so the backing edge doesn't show from the front. Use a point turner—not your scissors—to gently coax the corners into shape. Carefully turn in the raw edges at the opening and hand-sew or fuse together with narrow strips of fusible web. If you added a layer of batting, stitch through all layers around the outer edge of the oval. If desired, quilt the layers together using a diagonal grid of stitching across the oval. ❖

A Linty Picker-Upper

Because you are working with linen, your cutting surface is sure to be covered with bits of stray threads and scraps. Keep an adhesive lint roller in your sewing room to roll up those pesky bits. It's a good idea to remove any stray threads on both sides of the place mat before you turn it right side out, particularly if your fabrics are a lighter color. The interfacing on the wrong side will help mask show-through, but it may not be enough to hide any dark threads that might get trapped inside.

Spring Is Welcome Here

Colorful tulips waving in the breeze are a sure sign of spring. These appliquéd blooms top an easy-to-stitch banner with ribbons to flutter freely.

DESIGN BY JULIE WEAVER

Project Specifications

Banner Size: 25 x 54 inches

Materials

- ½ yard 54-inch-wide small floral print for appliqué background panel
- ⅝ yard 54-inch-wide small check for banner strips
- ⅝ yard 54-inch-wide plaid for banner strips
- 1⅔ yards 44/45-inch-wide coordinating print for lining fabric
- 7 x 20-inch piece of pink tone-on-tone batik print for tulips
- 12 x 14-inch piece of medium fern green tone-on-tone print for leaves A and B
- 10 x 14-inch piece of light fern green tone-on-tone print for tulip stems
- 9½ yards 1-inch-wide wire-edged ribbon
- Paper-backed fusible web
- Press cloth
- Seam sealant
- All-purpose sewing thread to match fabrics
- Basic sewing tools and equipment

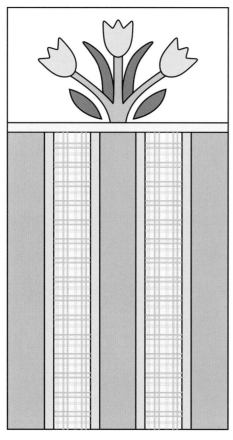

Fig. 1
Banner Assembly

Instructions

Project Note: *All seam allowances are ½ inch wide.*

Step 1. From the small floral print, cut a 17 x 26-inch rectangle. From the green-and-white checked fabric, cut three 6 x 39-inch strips. From the green-and-white plaid fabric, cut two 6 x 39-inch strips for the banner and one 6 x 24-inch strip, for a hanging sleeve.

Step 2. Enlarge the templates on page 34 as directed. Trace the required number of leaves and the stem onto the paper side of the fusible web. Leave ½ inch of space between pieces. Cut out each shape with a ¼-inch-wide margin beyond the traced lines. Following the manufacturer's directions, apply the shapes to the wrong side of the appropriately colored green fabric. Cut out on the traced lines.

Step 3. Trace the tulip template on page 34 onto the paper side of a 7 x 20-inch piece of fusible web leaving ¼ inch between the shapes. Following the manufacturer's directions, apply the fusible web to the wrong side of the pink fabric and cut out the tulips on the lines.

Step 4. Remove the paper backing from each appliqué. Referring to Fig. 1, position the appliqués on the 17 x 26-inch print rectangle in numerical order. When pleased with the arrangement, fuse the pieces in place following the manufacturer's directions. Protect the bottom of the iron by using a press cloth.

Step 5. Do a hand or machine blanket stitch over the appliqué edges using matching thread. Note: Use buttonhole twist and a large-eyed needle for more stitch definition whether stitching by hand or machine.

Step 6. Sew each 6-inch-wide plaid strip to a checked strip. Press the seams open. Arrange these pieces with the remaining checked piece and sew together to complete the lower section of the banner. Press the seams open.

Step 7. From the wire-edged ribbon, cut four 39-inch-long pieces. Remove the wire from both edges by pulling it out. Center a ribbon over each long seam line on the lower banner and stitch in place along both long edges.

Step 8. Sew the appliquéd upper panel to one short edge of the lower banner section. Press the seam open. Cut a 26-inch-long piece of ribbon, remove the wires, center over the seam and stitch in place.

Step 9. Fold the 6-inch-wide strip for the hanging sleeve in half lengthwise with wrong sides together and raw edges even. Stitch ¼ inch from the short ends. Turn the strip right side out and press. Center the strip on the right side of the banner at the upper edge and baste in place.

Step 10. Working on a large, flat surface, pin the banner to the lining with right sides together around the outer edges. Make sure the lining is smooth and wrinkle free. Stitch ¼ inch from the raw edges, leaving

a 6-inch-long opening in one side for turning. Trim the lining even with the banner raw edges.

Step 11. Turn the banner right side out through the opening and press, turning in the opening edges. Slipstitch the opening edges together. On the back of the banner, slipstitch the lower edge of the hanging sleeve to the lining only.

Step 12. Cut the remaining ribbon into four equal lengths. Leaving the wires intact, place two pieces of ribbon together and tie a bow. Fluff the four loops of the bow until you are pleased with how they look. Trim the ribbon edges at a 45-degree angle and treat the cut ends with seam sealant to prevent fraying.

Repeat with the remaining two pieces of ribbon. Pin or hand-tack the ribbon bows in place at the outer edges of the completed banner. Pin or tack in place on the right side of the banner. ❖

Make It Yours

Use the tulip appliqués to create a smaller wall hanging or pillow that finishes to 14 x 18 inches (Fig. 2). Use ¼-inch-wide seams.

1. Use the appliqué templates at half their original size. Prepare and appliqué the tulips and leaves as directed above to an 8½ x 12½-inch background panel.

2. Add a narrow inner border (cut 1½ inches wide) to the short ends, and then the long edges of the appliquéd panel. Add an outer border (cut 2½ inches wide).

3. Layer with batting and backing and quilt as desired (use a layer of muslin for the backing if you are making a quilted pillow top).

4. For a small quilt, bind the outer edges with a contrasting or matching binding. For a pillow, cut a backing the same size as the quilted pillow front. Sew together, leaving a 6-inch-long opening for turning. Turn right side out.

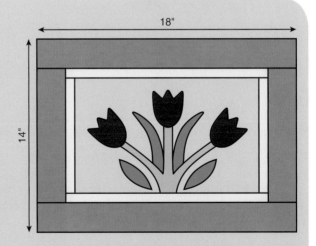

Fig. 2
Add borders to appliquéd panel
for small quilt or pillow cover.

5. Make a muslin pillow cover the same size as the pillow. Stuff with polyester fiberfill to the desired fullness and stitch the opening closed. Insert the quilted pillow cover and slipstitch the opening closed.

Keep It Clean

If you are going to hang your banner outside, consider treating it with a coat of spray-on fabric protector such as Scotchgard. Test first on the fabric and ribbon scraps to make sure it won't stain them.

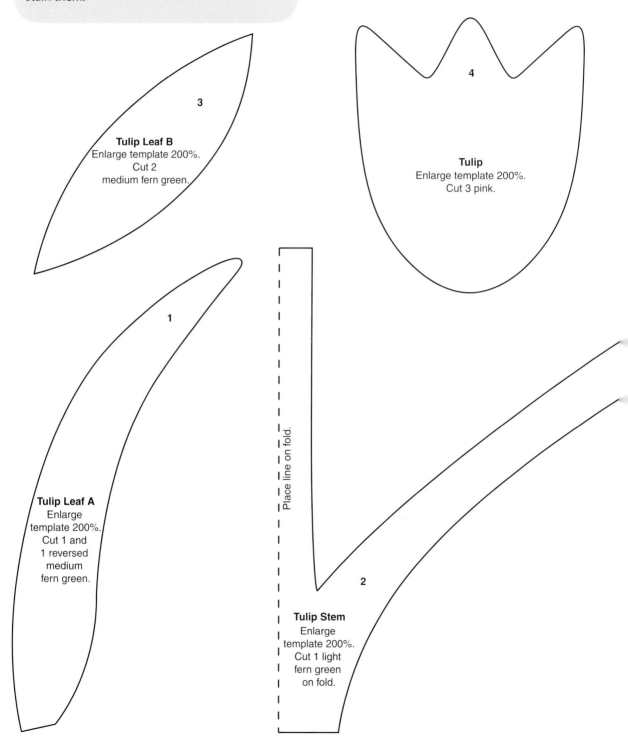

3

Tulip Leaf B
Enlarge template 200%.
Cut 2
medium fern green.

4

Tulip
Enlarge template 200%.
Cut 3 pink.

1

Tulip Leaf A
Enlarge
template 200%.
Cut 1 and
1 reversed
medium
fern green.

Place line on fold.

2

Tulip Stem
Enlarge
template 200%.
Cut 1 light
fern green
on fold.

Easter Bonnet Handbag

Turn a vintage straw hat upside down; add a bit of inner padding, a drawstring liner, a handle and some pretty trim. You'll have a one-of-a-kind handbag that will surely turn heads. Use similar techniques to turn a basket into a summer handbag with a few stitches and a little glue.

DESIGN BY LUCY B. GRAY

Project Specifications

Purse Size: Varies based on size of vintage hat used

Materials

- Vintage straw hat with deep crown and narrow brim, in good condition
- Gently used skirt or shirt in vintage floral print (or ⅓ yard of similar fabric) for outer liner
- Gently used skirt or shirt with long sleeves in coordinating plaid (or ½ yard of similar fabric) for inner liner
- Scrap of color-coordinated leather or imitation-suede fabric
- Thin polyester fleece for bag interlining and padding
- ⅔ yard ⅝-inch-wide fabric-covered boning for handle
- 1⅓ yards of ¼-inch-diameter cord for handle
- 3¼ yards of color-coordinated rattail cord for drawstring
- 12 small shirt buttons
- Button and carpet thread
- Rotary cutter, mat and ruler
- Spray-on fabric protector
- Quick-drying fabric glue
- Masking tape
- Leather and curved hand-sewing needles
- Old ribbons, fabric flowers, etc., for embellishment (optional)
- Basic sewing tools and equipment
- Craft scissors

Instructions

Step 1. Make any minor repairs required on the hat, if necessary.

Step 2. Cut pieces of polyester fleece to fit inside the hat and fit them to shape as needed with snipping, overlapping and trimming. Add two circles of fleece to the bottom. Use a curved needle to anchor the fleece to the hat interior (Photo 1). Add a layer of fleece to the hat underbrim in the same manner.

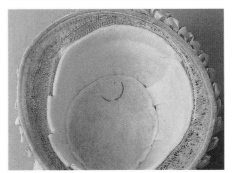

Photo 1

Step 3. Choose a fabric for the hat underbrim and apply several coats of fabric protector to keep it clean during use. Follow the directions on the can and allow to dry thoroughly between applications.

Step 4. Using rotary-cutting tools, cut 4-inch-wide bias strips from the garment pieces (or other fabric) to cover the hat underbrim. To make a strip of bias long enough to fit around the hat brim, it may be necessary to cut several shorter pieces—from a salvaged sleeve for example—and then sew them together with bias seams to make one long piece (Fig. 1).

Photo 2

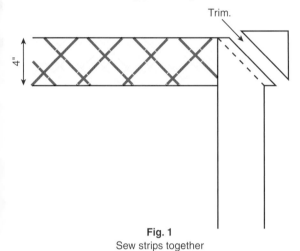

Fig. 1
Sew strips together
with bias seams.

Step 5. Serge- or zigzag-finish one long edge of the bias strip. Machine-baste along the opposite edge and draw up the bobbin thread to softly gather the edge (Fig. 2).

Fig. 2
Machine-baste ¹/₄" from edge.

Step 6. Refer to Photo 2. With the wrong side out, hand-overcast the finished edge of the bias strip to the outer edge of the hat brim. Next, turn the binding over the brim and anchor the gathered edge to the inside of the crown with pins. Adjust the gathers as needed for a snug, taut fit over the underside of the brim. Using carpet thread and a curved needle, stitch the lower edge of the bias strip to the inside of the crown, pushing the needle through to the outside and back with large backstitches (Photo 3). Use thread that matches the hat color and make

Photo 3

your stitches on the outside of the hat as discreet as possible. You can add a ribbon embellishment later to cover the stitching if you wish.

Step 7. Refer to Fig. 3 on page 38 for this step. For the double-layer liner, first measure the circumference of the hat around the inside edge of the underbrim and add 1 inch for seam allowances (for this hat 22 inches plus 1 inch). Decide how tall you want the liner. (It should extend several inches above the hat brim to allow for soft gathers and a roomy interior. The line for the hat shown extends about 6 inches above the hat brim.) To this measurement, add 2 inches for the drawstring casing at the upper edge (12½ inches plus 2 inches for this hat). Use these two measurements to cut a rectangle from the plaid liner fabric (for this hat 14½ x 23 inches). For the floral liner, cut a rectangle that is 2 inches smaller in the smaller dimension (12½ x 23 inches in this case). For the bottom of the liner, cut a circle of the plaid that is 1 inch larger than the diameter of the crown (5 inches plus 1 inch in this example).

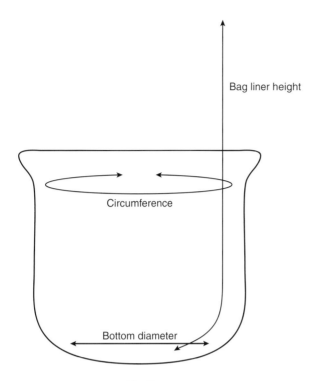

Fig. 3
Measure hat for liner dimensions.

inner liner. Place the plaid inner liner inside the outer floral liner with wrong sides together and the seams opposite (not on top of each other) and the lower edges of the liners aligned. Stitch together ⅜ inch from the lower raw edges. At the upper edge, turn the plaid inner liner to the outside over the edge of the floral outer liner and press. Beginning at the drawstring opening, stitch ¼ inch from the upper and lower edges of the plaid liner to form the drawstring casing. Machine-baste another row of stitches for gathering ¼ inch from the lower edge of the liner tube through both layers (Fig. 5). Note: If your vintage hat has a label, give credit to its designer by stitching the label to the liner circle—and add your own label too to signify your joint effort.

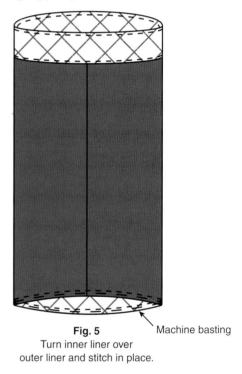

Fig. 5
Turn inner liner over
outer liner and stitch in place.

Machine basting

Step 8. Apply several coats of fabric protector to the right side of the liner pieces following manufacturer's directions. Allow to dry thoroughly between applications.

Step 9. Fold the plaid inner layer of lining in half lengthwise with right sides together. Using a ½-inch-wide seam allowance, stitch as shown, leaving an opening in the seam for the drawstring insertion. Press the seam open. Repeat with the outer layer but stitch the entire seam (Fig. 4).

Step 10. Turn under and press ½ inch at the upper edge of the plaid

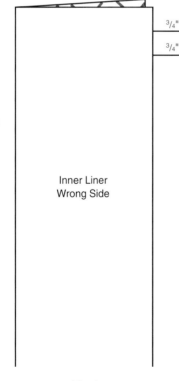

¾"

¾"

Inner Liner
Wrong Side

Fig. 4
Leave an opening in seam
for drawstring.

Step 11. Draw up the bobbin thread at the lower edge of the liner to fit the outer edge of the bottom circle. Pin the right side of the circle to the right side of the inner layer of the liner so the raw edges of the seam allowance will lie against the inside of the bag, not the lining interior. Stitch ½ inch from the raw edges, twice for stability. Anchor the liner to the hat bottom by sewing several small buttons spaced around the bottom perimeter inside the liner. Hand-sew through the hat layers with thread that matches the hat material.

Step 12. For the rigid handle, cut a 22-inch-long piece of ⅝-inch-wide boning. Place the boning face down on the wrong side of a 1¼-inch-wide strip of the floral liner fabric and wrap the raw edges over the boning. Use fast-drying fabric glue to attach the edges to the back of the boning strip. **Note:** *You can make and substitute a long 1-inch-wide fabric strap for the rigid bag handle if you wish.* Make a fabric tube of the desired length for the strap and anchor it to the inside of the bag before securing the lining around the inner edge of the hat brim (see below).

Step 13. Cut two 24-inch-long pieces of the ¼-inch-diameter cord and a 3 x 24-inch bias strip of the plaid lining fabric. Apply several coats of fabric protector to the right side of the plaid strip and allow to dry thoroughly between applications.

Step 14. With one piece of cord ¾ inch from one long edge on the wrong side of the bias strip, wrap the strip around it. Place the covered boning strip on top, covering the raw edge, and snug it up against the cord. Attach the zipper foot to your machine, adjust the needle position

Photo 4

and stitch the edge of the boning to the corded strip. Add the remaining strip of cord in the same manner, tucking the raw edge under the boning. Stitch in place (Photo 4). Trim as needed using craft scissors.

Step 15. Anchor the strap ends to the inside of the hat well below the junction of the hat brim and crown, using sturdy carpet and button thread and a leather sewing needle (available online from www.wanderingbull.com, if your fabric store doesn't carry them).

Step 16. Use small shirt buttons on the inside around the perimeter of the crown to anchor the liner to the upper edge of the bag and hide all raw edges (Photo 5). To determine the button placement, pull the lining straight up and fold it over on itself so you have clear access to the bag's interior. Place straight pins through the lining to

Photo 5

CONTINUED ON PAGE 47

Hunting for Handbag Components

Thrift and secondhand shops are great places to find wonderful old hats. They can cost pennies or much more, depending on their style and condition. This one was just $5.

• Look for a deep-crowned hat to make a roomy bag. Straw is wonderful for spring but consider other hat materials for other seasons. Look for hats that are in reasonably good condition without ravaged straw or serious dents in the crown that won't pop back out.

• When you've found the right hat, continue the search for the other components—secondhand garments in fabrics that coordinate for the liner and trim. Secondhand garments are perfect to cut up for a project like this. Skirts and dresses provide the largest pieces of fabric to work with, but you can also cut up long-sleeved shirts and piece the fabric sections together if needed.

• While you're looking for the components, keep an eye out for ribbons, flowers and other embellishments that you can add to the hat if it is not already suitably decorated. Your own stash of ribbons, fabric scraps, and garments you love but no longer wear are also great sources for the components you'll need for this bag.

• Before you begin your project, launder the garments if needed and then cut them apart along the seam lines. Cut away and discard the seam allowances and snip off any buttons or other trim to use later if desired. Press the pieces to remove wrinkles.

Chenille Fancy Footstool

Chenille By The Inch makes a wonderful embellishment on this little footstool. This innovative product makes it easy to re-create the vintage look of Grandma's chenille bedspread without the need to stack, stitch and cut layers of fabric to make the chenille strips.

DESIGN BY CAROL ZENTGRAF

Project Specifications
Footstool Size: 13 x 10 x 10 inches

Materials
- 13 x 10 x 10-inch oval wooden footstool
- ¾ yard 60-inch-wide chenille fabric
- 10 x 13-inch piece of 2-inch-thick upholstery foam
- High-loft batting
- Tear-away stabilizer
- 1⅛ yards of ball fringe
- Chenille By The Inch in pink, lavender, turquoise and green
- Chenille By The Inch cutting guide
- Chenille brush
- Spray bottle of water
- Rotary cutter and mat
- Staple gun
- Electric bread knife
- Permanent fabric adhesive
- Basic sewing tools and equipment

Instructions
Step 1. From the chenille fabric, cut one 8½-inch-wide strip across the width of the fabric for the skirt. Turn the footstool upside down on the wrong side of the remaining fabric and trace around the top, allowing a 3-inch-wide margin of fabric all around. Cut out 3

inches beyond the drawn line. Cut a piece of batting to match the chenille oval.

Step 2. Trace the outline of the footstool top onto the upholstery foam. Use the electric knife to cut the oval from the foam. Glue the foam to the top of the stool. Use the knife to slightly round off (bevel) the upper edge of the foam.

Step 3. Trace the design template for the footstool on page 43 onto tear-away stabilizer. Center the design on the right side of the chenille fabric oval and pin in place.

Pillow Time

Use a portion of the same design and the same technique to make a matching pillow. To make a pillow cover for a 14-inch-diameter pillow form, you will need ½ yard of chenille fabric and 1¼ yards of ball fringe.

1. For the pillow cover, cut two 15-inch-diameter circles from the chenille (see Cut a Perfect Circle on page 43) and apply the design (large flower and leaves) as directed for the footstool.

2. Baste the header of the ball fringe to the circle, then add the remaining circle with right sides facing. Stitch the circles together, leaving a 6-inch opening for turning.

3. Turn right side out, insert the pillow form and slipstitch the opening closed on the back of the pillow.

Step 4. Remove the stabilizer that comes on the back of each color of the Chenille By The Inch. Following the manufacturer's instructions, use the cutting guide and a rotary cutter to cut the strips between the stitching lines.

Step 5. Align the stitching on the chenille strips with the marked design lines on the stabilizer and sew the chenille strips in place, overlapping the strip ends ¼ inch as needed (Fig.1). Lightly spray the chenille trim with water. Use the chenille brush and brush the trim until it's fluffy.

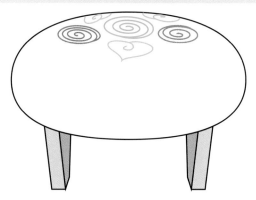

Fig. 2
Staple chenille oval with batting
to edge of footstool.

Fig. 1
Arrange chenille strips
on pattern drawn on stabilizer.
Stitch in place.

Step 6. Place the chenille oval right side up on top of the oval of batting. Treating the two pieces as one, center the layers on top of the foam on the stool. Use the staple gun to attach the edges to the stool edge of the stool (Fig. 2).

Step 7. Serge- or zigzag-finish one long edge of the chenille panel for the footstool skirt. With right sides

facing, sew or serge the short edges of the panel together ½ inch from the raw edges. Turn under and press ½ inch at the serge-finished edge of the chenille tube you've created and topstitch in place.

Step 8. Set the machine for a basting-length stitch. Stitch ⅜ inch from the upper raw edge of the skirt. Draw up the bobbin thread from both ends to gather the upper edge to fit snugly around the padded and covered stool edge. Distribute the gathers evenly around the stool and pin in place, making sure that the skirt lower edge is an even distance from the floor all around. Attach the gathered edge of the skirt to the stool edge with closely spaced staples along the inner edge of the serge-finishing stitches.

Step 9. Glue ball fringe in place, covering the upper edge of the skirt and the staples. ❖

Chenille Fancy Footstool Template
Actual Size

Cut a Perfect Circle

1. With the wrong side out, fold the fabric in half and then in half again with folded edges even. Place on a padded surface and make sure it is wrinkle-free and all edges are aligned.

2. Tie a long piece of string around a sharp pencil or fabric marker.

3. Determine the radius of the circle (half the diameter) and add ½ inch for a seam allowance (for a 14-inch finished diameter, the radius plus seam allowance is 7½ inches). Measure this distance from the pencil and insert a straight pin through the string at that point.

4. Insert the pin into the folded corner of the fabric square and hold the pencil or marker perpendicular to the fabric as you draw the circle (Fig. 3).

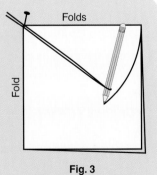

Fig. 3
Draw a quarter-circle on a folded fabric square.

Hearts-All-Around Neckroll

Pieced hearts and lace trim lend a romantic note to this pretty pillow. Coordinating purchased cording and tassels add the finishing flourishes.

DESIGN BY PAMELA LINDQUIST

Project Specifications

Pillow Size: 6 x 18 inches

Materials

Project Note: *All yardages are for 44/45-inch-wide fabrics.*

- ¼ yard pink tone-on-tone fabric for the pieced upper heart section
- ¼ yard pink solid for the pieced lower heart section
- ⅜ yard cream tone-on-tone print for the heart block background
- ⅝ yard floral paisley print for the borders and bolster ends
- 1⅜ yards narrow lace trim
- 1⅜ yards ¼-inch-diameter pink corded piping for inner edge trim
- 1⅜ yards ½-inch-diameter pink corded piping for outer edge trim
- 6 x 18-inch bolster pillow form
- 2 (1-inch-diameter) decorative or self-covered buttons
- 2 decorative tassels
- Optional: Buttonhole twist or carpet thread for gathered end treatment
- All-purpose threads to match fabrics
- Pencil
- Rotary cutter, mat and ruler
- Zipper or piping foot
- Basic sewing tools and equipment

Instructions

Project Notes: *Preshrink all fabrics. Strip lengths are based on 42 inches of usable width after preshrinking. If fabrics are narrower, you may need additional fabric. Measurements include ¼-inch-wide seam allowances unless otherwise stated.*

Step 1. From the pink tone-on-tone print, cut two strips each 2½ x 42 inches; crosscut (30) 2½-inch squares. From the pink solid print, cut two strips each 2½ x 42 inches; crosscut 15 rectangles each 2½ x 4½ inches. From the cream tone-on-tone print, cut two strips each 1¼ x 42 inches; crosscut (60) 1¼-inch squares. Cut two strips each 2 ½ x 42 inches; crosscut (30) 2½-inch squares. From the floral paisley print, cut two strips each 3¾ x 20 inches and two strips each 4½ x 20 inches.

Make It Yours

For a more traditional Valentine pillow, substitute reds and deeper pinks for the hearts and choose a bolder, more graphic print for the borders and pillow ends.

Step 2. Using a sharp pencil and ruler, draw a diagonal line from corner to corner on the wrong side of each 1¼-inch cream square. Repeat with the 2½-inch cream squares.

Step 3. With right sides together, place a marked 2½-inch cream square face down at one end of a 2½ x 4½-inch pink rectangle. Stitch on the marked line. Trim the excess fabric ¼ inch from the stitching. Press the seam toward the cream triangle that remains. Repeat at the opposite end of the triangle. Repeat with the remaining cream squares and pink rectangles to make a total of 15 lower units (Fig. 1).

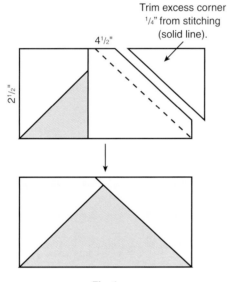

Fig. 1
Make 15 lower units.

Step 4. Repeat Step 2 using the 1¼-inch cream squares and the 2½-inch pink squares to make a total of 30 quarter-heart units (Fig. 2).

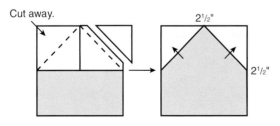

Fig. 2
Make 30 upper units.

Step 5. Sew the units from Step 4 together in pairs to make 15 half-heart upper units. Press the seam allowances to one side. Sew an upper heart unit to a lower unit to make 13 heart blocks (Fig. 3). You should have 2 each of the upper and lower halves left.

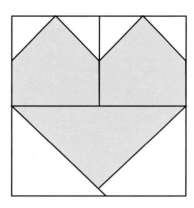

Fig. 3
Make 13 Heart blocks.

Step 6. Arrange the heart blocks and remaining half-heart units in three vertical rows as shown in Fig. 4, beginning and ending the first and third rows with the half-heart units. Sew the blocks together in vertical rows and press the seams in opposite directions from row to row. Sew the rows together and press the seams in one direction.

Fig. 4
Pillow Cover Assembly

Step 7. Machine-baste lace trim to the long edges of the patchwork panel. Position the narrow corded piping at the long edges and machine-baste in place, using a zipper or piping foot to stitch close to the piping.

Step 8. With right sides together, sew a 3¾ x 20-inch strip of floral paisley print to each long edge of the patchwork using the zipper foot to stitch close to the corded piping. Stitch from the patchwork side so you can see the stitching that holds the piping in place. *Note: It may feel like you are "crowding" the piping as you stitch but that is correct.* Press the seams toward the patchwork panel.

Step 9. Fold the pillow cover in half crosswise with right sides together and the 19-inch-long raw edges even. Stitch ¼ inch from the edges and finger-press the seam open.

Step 10. Turn the pillow cover right side out. Cut two 22-inch-long pieces of ½-inch-diameter pink corded piping. Using a ½-inch-wide seam allowance, sew the piping to the raw edges of each end of the pillow cover, angling the piping ends off the edge where they meet for a neat finish (Fig. 5).

Fig. 5
Overlap corded piping ends.
Trim even with pillow cover edge.

Step 11. For the pillow ends, fold each 4½ x 20-inch strip of floral paisley print in half crosswise with right sides together and short raw edges even. Stitch ¼ inch from the raw edges.

Step 12. Turn under and press ½ inch at one raw edge on each end piece and topstitch ¼ inch from the folded edge.

Step 13. With right sides together, raw edges even and seam lines matching, pin one floral paisley print end piece to one open end of the pillow cover. Stitch ½ inch from the long edges. Repeat at the opposite end of the pillow cover.

Step 14. Insert the pillow form.

Step 15. Thread a hand-sewing needle with strong thread (buttonhole twist or carpet thread). Make running stitches along the finished edge of each end piece. Pull up the thread to gather and draw the ends into the center. Tie off securely. Sew a large covered or purchased button in the center at each end of the finished neckroll. Attach a tassel to each button. ❖

EASTER BONNET HANDBAG CONTINUED FROM PAGE 39

the hat's exterior at the crown-brim juncture. Sew the buttons in place, spacing them two or three finger widths apart. Use thread that matches the hat exterior. Add buttons to any area where the liner pulls away at the crown. Add a button at each strap end as well.

Step 17. For the drawstring, cut three pieces of rattail cord each 36 inches long. Braid them tightly together. Secure the ends with masking tape. Fasten a safety pin through one taped end and thread the braided cord through the drawstring casing. Open the drawstring bag to its fullest and tie the braided cord ends together with a square knot, about 8 inches from the casing opening. Remove the masking tape; unbraid the loose ends of the cord below the knot to form a six-thread tassel and trim the ends even. Wrap the tassel tightly just below the square knot with a small piece of leather or imitation suede and glue it with quick-drying fabric glue. Add a button or bead to the leather wrap if you wish.

Step 18. Embellish the hat exterior below the brim with a fresh ribbon and a silk flower. These can be rescued vintage pieces or new ones from your stash. Apply ribbons with small dots of fabric glue, reinforced here and there with tiny stitches in matching thread. Attach flowers and leaves permanently with fabric glue. ❖

Summer Sizzlers

With the sun at full strength, summer days stretch into the evening. That means there are more daytime hours to enjoy sewing these easy projects for your home and wardrobe.

Sailing Through Summer

The trio of patriotic sailboats on this welcome banner signals that summer is here!

DESIGN BY ANNABELLE KELLER

Project Specifications
Banner Size: 20½ x 32½ inches

Materials
Project Note: Yardage is for 44/45-inch-wide tone-on-tone cotton prints.

- 1 yard white for welcome panel, sails and backing
- 1 yard dark blue for sashing, borders and binding
- ⅓ yard red for letters, boat hulls and flags
- ¼ yard light blue for sky and water
- ¼ yard paper-backed fusible web
- 20½ x 32½-inch piece of fusible batting
- ¼ yard tear-away stabilizer
- ¾ yard medium-width silver metallic rickrack
- All-purpose threads to match fabrics
- Monofilament nylon thread
- 2 (1-inch) ball knobs with ½-inch holes
- 21¾-inch-long piece ½-inch-diameter dowel
- Silver metallic spray paint
- 1⅓ yards ³⁄₁₆-inch-diameter metallic silver cord
- Tacky craft glue
- Pencil
- Template plastic
- Rotary cutter, mat and ruler
- Sheet of fine sandpaper
- Basic sewing tools and equipment

Instructions
Project Note: Seam allowances are ¼ inch wide unless otherwise noted. Wash, dry and press all fabrics before cutting.

Step 1. From the dark blue print, cut two 2½ x 8½-inch sashing strips, one 2½ x 28½-inch sashing strip, two 2½ x 16½-inch border strips and two 2½ x 32½-inch border strips. For the binding, cut three 2½ x 42-inch strips.

Step 2. From the white print, cut one piece 6½ x 28½ inches, one 20½ x 32½-inch piece for the backing and one 5 x 20-inch strip for the hanging sleeve.

Step 3. Enlarge all templates on page 54 as directed. Trace each enlarged template onto template plastic and cut out carefully. Trace the letters onto the paper side of an 8 x 17-inch piece of fusible web. Apply to the wrong side of the red fabric following manufacturer's directions and cut out. Set aside. Trace around the templates for the sailboat block on the wrong side of the appropriate-color fabrics. Trace the number indicated on the templates for each piece. *Note: To keep the fabric from slipping while tracing around the templates, place the fabric on sandpaper.*

Step 4. Working in a well-ventilated area, apply silver spray paint to the knobs and dowel, and set aside to dry.

Step 5. Refer to Fig. 1 for this step and Steps 6–8. Pair the flags with right sides together and stitch, leaving an opening in the short edge for turning. Clip the corners, trim the seams to a scant ⅛ inch, turn right side out and press.

Step 6. Arrange the sail and sky pieces as shown in Fig. 1 and sew together. Press the seams toward the sky. Arrange the hull and water sections and sew together. Press the seams toward the hulls.

Step 7. Center an 8-inch length of silver rickrack on each sail and tuck the short unfinished edge of a flag underneath. Pin in place. Stitch the rickrack in place using monofilament thread and catching the flag in the stitching. Trim the rickrack even with the edges of the sail unit.

Step 8. Sew the sail/sky and hull/water sections together to complete each of the three blocks. Press the seam toward the hull.

Step 9. Refer to Fig. 2 for this step and Steps 10–13. Arrange the blocks with the 2½ x 8½-inch dark blue sashing strips between them and sew together. Press the seams toward the sashing strips. Add the

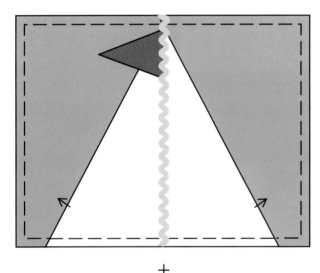

Fig. 1
Sew pieces together to make 3 blocks.

Make It Yours

Choose entirely different colors to make this banner for any time of the year. Consider using these easy blocks to make a quilt for a little boy's room.

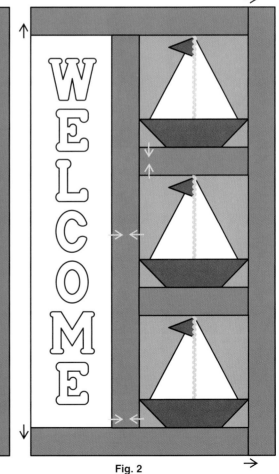

Fig. 2
Banner Assembly

2½ x 28½-inch sashing strip to the left-hand edge of the panel. Press the seam toward the sashing strip. Set aside.

Step 10. Remove the backing paper from the letters. Center the C vertically and horizontally in the white strip and fuse in place. Position the remaining letters ⅝ inch apart, except for the O and M, which should be spaced ⅜ inch apart. When satisfied with the placement, fuse the remaining letters in place following manufacturer's instructions.

Step 11. Position tear-away stabilizer behind each letter and pin in place. With red thread, adjust the machine for a narrow satin-stitch and stitch around the raw edges of each letter. Pivot as necessary for smooth stitching.

Step 12. Sew the welcome panel to the left-hand edge of the long blue sashing. Press the seam toward the sashing.

Step 13. Sew the short borders to the top and bottom edges of the hanging and press the seams toward the borders. Add the long borders in the same manner.

Step 14. Position the fusible batting on the wrong side of the white backing and arrange the pieced banner on top. Fuse the layers together following the manufacturer's directions.

Step 15. Sew the binding strips together using bias seams to make one long piece. Press the seams open. Turn one short end under at a 45-degree angle and trim, leaving a ¼-inch-wide allowance. Fold the strip in half lengthwise with wrong sides together and press (Fig. 3). Beginning on one long edge of the banner, pin the binding to the banner.

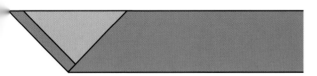

Fig. 3
Fold and press binding strip.

Step 16. Stitch the binding to the banner using ³⁄₈-inch-wide seams and mitering the corners as you reach them. Wrap the binding to the back of the banner and slipstitch in place.

Step 17. To quilt, machine stitch in the ditch of the seams in each block. Stitch ¼ inch from each seam line in the sashing and border strips. Stitch ¼ inch and ½ inch from the seam lines in the white WELCOME strip.

Step 18. Make a double narrow hem at each short end of the 5 x 20-inch white strip for the hanging sleeve. Fold the strip in half lengthwise with wrong sides together and stitch ¼ inch from the raw edges. Center the seam on the back of the tube and press the seam open. Press both folded edges to crease.

Step 19. Position one creased edge just below the inner edge of the binding and slipstitch in place.

Step 20. Pin a ¼-inch deep tuck in only the upper layer of the hanging sleeve as shown in Fig. 4 and then sew the lower edge of the sleeve to the quilt backing only. Remove the pins. This creates a little slack in the sleeve to accommodate the strain of the hanging rod.

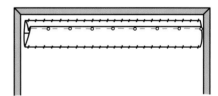

Fig. 4
Pin a narrow tuck (¹⁄₄") in upper layer
of sleeve. Slipstitch upper and lower edges
of sleeve to backing.

Step 21. Insert the silver dowel through the hanging sleeve. Measure 12 inches from each end of the metallic cord and tie once around the dowel ½ inch from the dowel ends. Glue the knots to the back side of the dowel. Glue ball knobs to the dowel ends. Knot the cord ¾ inch from the ends. Apply glue to the knots and untwist the cord below the knots. ❖

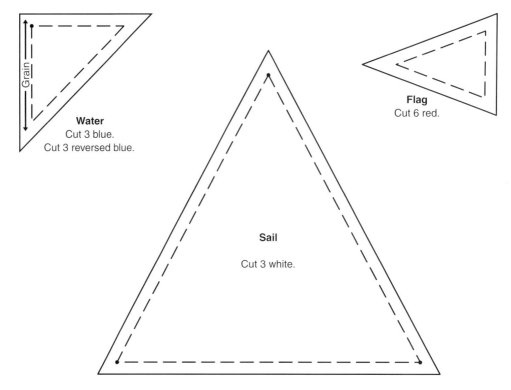

Water
Cut 3 blue.
Cut 3 reversed blue.

Grain

Flag
Cut 6 red.

Sail

Cut 3 white.

Templates for Sailing Through Summer
Enlarge 200%

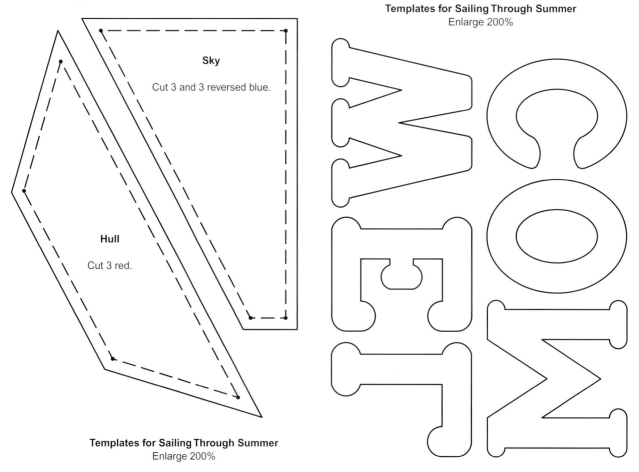

Templates for Sailing Through Summer
Enlarge 200%

Sky

Cut 3 and 3 reversed blue.

Hull

Cut 3 red.

Templates for Sailing Through Summer
Enlarge 200%

Trace 2 Es and 1 each of the remaining letters.

Pajama Party

Choose several sweet cotton prints that make you smile and piece them together to make playful pajamas for lounging and dreaming on hot summer nights.

DESIGN BY NANCY FIEDLER

Project Specifications

Pajama Set Size: Your size

Materials

- Pajama pattern of your choice with pull-on bottoms and camisole top
- ¾ yard each of eight different 44/45-inch-wide cotton prints
- 1 yard ¼-inch-wide ribbon
- 2¼ yards 1-inch-wide eyelet trim
- Pattern tracing paper
- Notions as listed on the pattern envelope
- All-purpose thread to match fabrics
- 4mm twin sewing machine needle
- Basic sewing tools and equipment

Instructions

Step 1. Wash and dry all fabrics to preshrink. Press to remove wrinkles.

Step 2. Cut out the pattern pieces in your size and make any fitting adjustments required for your figure.

Step 3. Draw a line from the center of the waistline edge of the pajama bottom front to the hem edge, making it parallel to the grainline and dividing the leg in half. Repeat with the pattern piece for the back leg pattern piece. For capri-length pajama bottoms, draw a new hemline 8 inches above the bottom edge of the front and back pattern pieces. Number the sections of each leg.

Step 4. Trace the front and back leg sections onto pattern tracing paper and add ⅝-inch-wide seam allowances to the center edge of each section. Draw crosswise grainlines on each piece (Fig. 1).

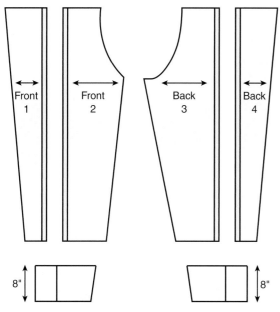

Fig. 1
Cut patterns apart and
add ⅝" seam allowances.
Number each piece and
label crosswise grainlines.

Step 5. On the camisole front pattern piece, draw a line parallel to the hemline approximately 8 inches above the lower edge. Draw another line parallel to the center front to divide the lower front section in half. Repeat with the back pattern piece. Refering to Fig. 2, trace the new pattern sections onto tracing paper, adding ⅝-inch-wide seam allowances.

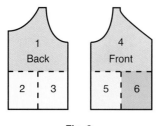

Fig. 2
Draw piecing lines on
camisole pattern pieces.

Step 6. Layer two of the fabrics with right sides together and cut out pajama bottom Section 1. Layer two different fabrics with right sides together and cut out Section 2. Continue in the same manner for Sections 3 and 4 so that all eight fabrics are used for the pajama bottom pieces.

Step 7. Cut camisole Sections 1 and 4 on the fold, cutting each from a different fabric. Cut two each of Sections 2, 3, 5 and 6, cutting each one from a different fabric.

Step 8. Cut the facings and straps from your choice of the remaining fabrics.

Step 9. Sew the front sections of the legs together using a ⅝-inch-wide seam. Serge- or zigzag-finish the seam edges together and press the seams toward the center front. Insert the 4mm twin needle, thread it and topstitch the seam allowances in place to create a mock flat-felled seam.

Step 10. Sew together the pieces for the lower front and back for the camisole in the same manner. Then sew the upper front and upper back to the lower pieced panels, press and topstitch as for the pajama bottoms.

Step 11. Construct the pajama bottoms following the pattern guidesheet. Serge-finish the lower edge of each pant leg and turn under along the serging; press. Or turn and press a double narrow hem.

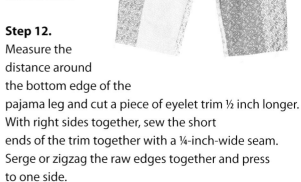

Step 12. Measure the distance around the bottom edge of the pajama leg and cut a piece of eyelet trim ½ inch longer. With right sides together, sew the short ends of the trim together with a ¼-inch-wide seam. Serge or zigzag the raw edges together and press to one side.

Step 13. Sew the eyelet trim in place by tucking its upper edge under the finished hem edge and edgestitching through all layers.

Step 14. Construct the camisole following the pattern directions. Prepare the facings as directed but turn under and press ⅝ inch along the lower edge of the assembled facing, clipping as needed for a smoothly turned edge. Pin the facing to the camisole neckline edge *with the right side of the facing against the wrong side of the camisole.* Stitch in place as directed, trim the seams to ¼ inch and turn to the right side of the camisole. Press.

Step 15. Stitch the facings to the camisole front and back along the lower turned edges.

Step 16. Hem the camisole and add eyelet trim to the lower edge as described above for the pajama bottoms.

Step 17. Tack an 18-inch-long piece of narrow ribbon to the center front seam of the pajama bottoms in the center of the waistline casing. Cut ends at a 45-degree angle. Tack a similar length to the center front of the camisole. Tie the ends in small bows and tack in place. ❖

Make It Yours

Make print-blocked pajamas from cozy flannel fabrics in fall or holiday colors. Use a pajama top pattern with long sleeves and do not shorten the pajama bottoms. When adapting the top pattern for the pieced sections, measure from the shoulder seam to the hemline and use ⅓ of this measurement for the length of the lower pieced sections. Divide the sleeve pattern in half lengthwise, drawing the line from the shoulder dot to the hem. Trace the new sections of each piece and add seam allowances. Cut each sleeve section from a different fabric so that each sleeve is made from two different fabrics and the right sleeve does not match the left sleeve. Adjust the pattern pieces first and take them to the fabric store to determine the required yardage for each piece.

Fat Quarter Confetti Jacket

Collect your favorite fat quarters and rip them into ribbons of colorful confetti to make a new fabric for this lightweight, summer shirt jacket. Raw edges and decorative stitching add to the fun of stitching up this wonderfully easy wearable.

DESIGN BY BARBARA WEILAND

Project Specifications

Jacket Size: Your size

Materials

- Loose-fitting shirt-jacket pattern in your size (with no center-back seam)
- 12–14 fat quarters (18 x 22-inch pieces) cotton batik; choose a multicolored print as the focal fabric and then select the other fat quarters in colors and prints that coordinate with it
- Lightweight, firmly woven, cotton or silk fabric for jacket foundation in the yardage given on pattern envelope plus ½ yard
- ½ yard coordinating fabric for facings and undercollar
- 1 fat quarter for edge finish on sleeves and hem
- Lightweight fusible interfacing in yardage given on pattern envelope
- ¼-inch-wide double-stick repositionable fusible tape
- Approximately 8 yards ⅜-inch-wide satin ribbon
- All-purpose thread to match fabrics
- Rayon embroidery thread to match fabrics
- Zigzag sewing machine with built-in or programmable decorative stitches
- Bobbin thread
- Buttons and notions as listed on pattern envelope

Make It Yours

For a dressier version of this technique, cut ⅝-inch-wide bias strips from lightweight silk taffeta and/or dupioni and apply side by side to a lightweight, firmly woven silk foundation. To attach the strips to the foundation, straight stitch through the center of each one. The edges will be free and won't ravel because they were cut on the bias.

Instructions

Step 1. Adjust the pattern pieces to fit your figure as needed.

Step 2. Measure and note the width and length of each of the following pattern pieces: front, back, sleeve, collar.

Step 3. From the foundation fabric, cut a rectangle 2 inches longer and wider than each of the above pattern pieces. For a shirt jacket you will have rectangles for two fronts, one back, one collar and two sleeves. You will cut the actual garment pieces after creating the fabric for each part of the jacket.

Step 4. Center each pattern piece on the appropriate rectangle and trace around it with a sharp pencil. Be sure to flip the sleeve and front patterns on the second rectangle for each one.

Step 5. Choose the fat quarter print for the front edge of the jacket and tear three 3-inch-wide strips, tearing across the 22-inch edge of the fat quarter. Tear one of the strips into two equal lengths. *Note: You may need to make an initial tear at the edge that was cut from the bolt before you measure and tear the 3-inch-wide pieces.* Tear four additional strips of the same width and set aside for the center strip in the sleeves, collar and jacket back.

Step 6. On the wrong side at one short end of two of the long strips, position ¼-inch-wide fusible tape. Lap this end over the short end on the right side of one of the short pieces and fuse to make a strip long enough to match the length of the rectangle for the jacket front edge (Fig. 1). Use this method to splice additional strips of other colors as needed to cover the jacket tracing on the foundation.

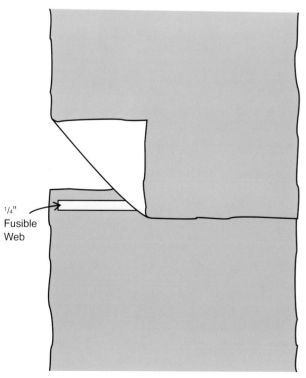

Fig. 1
Use fusible web to piece strips together as needed.

¼"
Fusible
Web

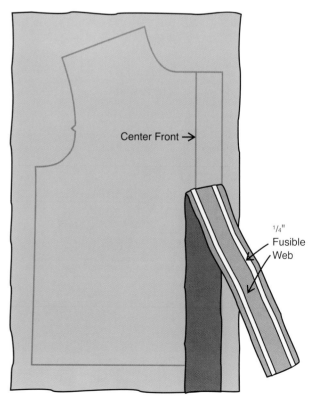

Center Front →

¼"
Fusible
Web

Fig. 2
Fuse strip to foundation
at front edge of jacket outline.

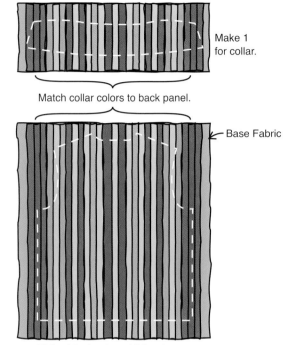

Make 1 for collar.

Match collar colors to back panel.

← Base Fabric

Make 1 for back and 2 for sleeves.

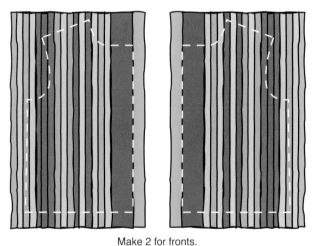

Make 2 for fronts.

Fig. 3
Fuse torn fabric strips to base rectangles.

Step 7. On the wrong side of one 3-inch-wide strip, apply fusible tape ¼ inch from the long torn edges. Position on a rectangle for the jacket front with one torn edge even with the line for the jacket front edge. Fuse in place (Fig. 2).

Step 8. Refer to Fig. 3 for Steps 8–14. Choose the next fabric color and tear 2½-inch-wide strips for each jacket front. Splice the strips as described in Step 6 as needed. Apply fusible web to the wrong side of the strip. Position it along the first strip with torn edges even and fuse in place.

Step 9. Continue in this manner until one rectangle for the jacket front is covered with fabric strips. For the second front, make a mirror-image rectangle.

Step 10. Tear ¾ x 22-inch strips from assorted fat quarters. Center and pin a contrasting strip of fabric on each strip on the rectangle for one jacket front.

Step 11. Using matching or contrasting rayon embroidery thread in the needle and bobbin thread in the bobbin, stitch through the center of the narrow strips. Use a variety of built-in decorative stitches for this stitching. Mirror-image the strips and stitching on the second jacket front rectangle.

Step 12. On the rectangles for the back and each sleeve, prepare, center and fuse a strip torn and set aside in Step 5. Add strips torn from other fabrics on either side of the center strip until the rectangle is covered.

Step 13. Using the rectangle for the back as a guide for color placement, center a strip on the collar rectangle to match the center back strip. Add remaining strips to match the color placement on the rectangle for the back.

Step 14. Position the pattern pieces on each strip-covered rectangle, pin in place and cut out. Transfer all construction markings. Remove the pattern pieces and staystitch the front and back necklines ½ inch from the raw edges.

Step 15. Refer to Fig. 4 for Steps 15 and 16. From three different fabrics, tear 2½- or 3-inch-wide strips for the cross bands on the jacket fronts and back. Position and fuse in place. Tear and center ¾-inch-wide strips on each band. Stitch in place with a decorative stitch of your choice.
Note: In the jacket shown, the narrower strip was not added to the uppermost strip to allow the pattern in the fabric to show to advantage.

Step 16. Apply fusible web to the wrong side of ribbon cut to fit between the bands on the jacket fronts and back. Center in the spaces between the three horizontal bands of color and fuse in place. You will add ribbon to the sleeves later. *Note: If you wish, you may use a decorative stitch to sew the ribbons in place after fusing.*

Step 17. Cut front and back neckline facings and the undercollar from the ½ yard of coordinating fabric and from fusible interfacing. Apply the interfacing to the wrong side of the facings following the manufacturer's directions.

Step 18. Assemble the jacket body, collar and facings following the pattern directions. Finish seam edges with serging, binding or zigzagging.

Step 19. Prepare each sleeve cap by machine basting ¼, ½ and ¾ inches from the raw edge between the notches. Machine baste the sleeve underarm seams.

Step 20. With right sides together, and dots and notches matching, pin the sleeves into the jacket armholes and adjust the easestitching to fit. *Place the pins along the seam line on the sleeve side of the seam, not across the seam line.* This makes it possible to try the jacket on and mark the positioning for the ribbons so they match the ribbon placement on the jacket front. Mark each ribbon position on each sleeve.

Step 21. Remove the sleeves from the jacket and remove the underarm seam basting.

Step 22. Apply fusible tape to ribbons cut to fit at the marked locations. Add ribbons between the first three ribbons, centering them in the space and fuse in place (Fig. 5).

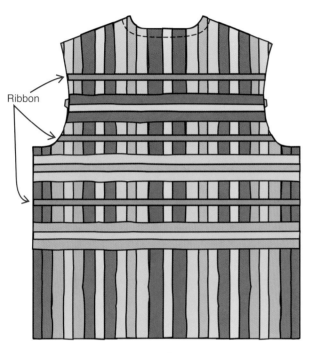

Ribbon

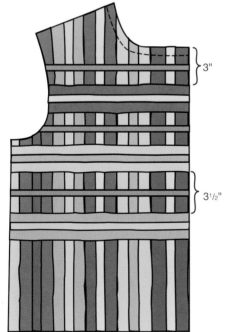

3"

3½"

Fig. 4
Add horizontal strips to fronts and back.

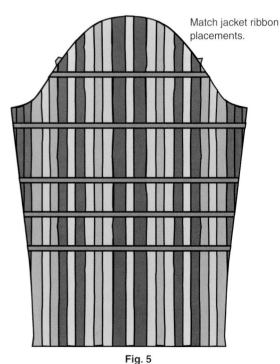

Match jacket ribbon placements.

Fig. 5
Sew ribbons to sleeve.

Step 23. Stitch the underarm seam and press open. Set the sleeves into the jacket armhole and finish the seam edges.

Step 24. Try on the jacket and mark the desired finished sleeve and jacket length.

Step 25. Trim away any hem allowance at the lower edge of the jacket and sleeves.

Step 26. From the fat quarter for the edge finish, cut three strips each 2½ x 22 inches. Sew the strips together with bias seams and press the seams open. Fold the strip in half with wrong sides together and press. With ¼ inch of the strip extending beyond the jacket front edges, pin and stitch the binding strip to the jacket right side. Stitch ⅜ inch from the raw edges. Press the binding toward the seam allowance, and then wrap it over the edge to the inside of the jacket. Turn the excess under at each front edge. From the right side, stitch in the ditch of the binding seam.

Step 27. For each sleeve, cut a strip 4½ inches wide and the length of the distance around the lower edge of the sleeve, plus 1½ inches. At one short end of each strip, turn under and press ½ inch.

Step 28. With right sides together and the pressed short end positioned at the underarm seam line,

pin a strip to the lower edge of each sleeve. Trim the excess strip, allowing for at least ½ inch to lap under the turned-and-pressed end of the band. Stitch ⅜ inch from the raw edges (Fig. 6).

Fig. 6
Sew band to lower edge
of sleeve.

Step 29. Press the band toward the seam allowance, and then wrap it to the inside over the seam edge, as if you were applying a binding. Pin in place and stitch in the ditch from the right side (Fig. 7).

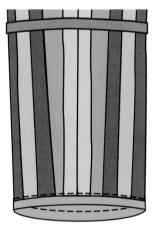

Fig. 7
Stitch in ditch of seam.

Step 30. Turn the sleeves inside out. Turn under and press ½ inch at the upper raw edge of the band. Pin in place, then slipstitch to the sleeve foundation. This allows you to wear the sleeves long or to roll the bottom edge back to expose the band.

Step 31. Make buttonholes and sew buttons in place on the jacket fronts. ❖

Silken Eye-Catchers

Give your eyeglasses a little TLC. Make one or both of these soft and luxurious cases for eye-catching fashion appeal. Use luscious silks and Asian-inspired prints or make a case to match each of the fabric handbags in your wardrobe.

DESIGNS BY PAM ARCHER

Project Specifications

Quilted Case Size: 4 x 7¾ inches

Pieced Case Size: 3½ x 6½ inches

Materials
Quilted Case

- ⅓ yard silk dupioni for lining
- ¼ yard silk dupioni for case exterior
- ⅓ yard fusible interfacing
- ⅓ yard cotton batting
- ⅓ yard rattail cord for drawstring
- 5 beads (to accommodate cord diameter)
- Air-soluble marking pen
- Seam sealant
- Temporary spray adhesive (optional)
- Point presser
- Pinking shears
- Tapestry needle

Pieced Case

Project Note: *Choose three coordinating fabrics.*

- 12 x 18-inch piece Fabric A for piecing
- 12 x 18-inch piece Fabric B for piecing
- ⅓ yard Fabric C for piecing and lining
- 9-inch-square piece lightweight cotton batting

All Projects

- All-purpose thread to match fabrics
- Rotary cutter, mat and ruler
- Pattern tracing cloth or tissue
- Basic sewing tools and equipment

Instructions

Project Note: *Use ¼-inch-wide seam allowances.*

Make It Yours

• Consider adding seed beads at the stitched intersections on the quilted cover.

• As an alternative, instead of quilting on the marked lines, couch some interesting yarn on each line. Lay the yarn in place on the line and adjust the machine for a zigzag stitch that is wide enough to capture the yarn under the stitching.

• Couch yarns over the seam lines of the patchwork case for added definition.

Quilted Case

Step 1. Press the fabrics to remove wrinkles. Cut two 7 x 8-inch rectangles from each of the following: silk for the exterior, fusible interfacing and cotton batting.

Step 2. Cut two 7 x 9-inch rectangles from the lining silk and from the fusible interfacing.

Step 3. Apply the interfacing to the wrong side of all four pieces of silk following the manufacturer's directions.

Step 4. Pin and baste cotton batting to the wrong side of the silk pieces for the outside of the case (or use temporary spray adhesive to adhere the layers).

Step 5. Using the air-soluble marker, draw quilting lines on the right side of the batting-backed silk. Beginning at the upper left corner, draw lines on the diagonal, spacing them 1 inch apart. Repeat from the upper right corner to create a diagonal grid.

Step 6. With matching thread, stitch along the marks to quilt the case cover pieces.

Step 7. Referring to Fig. 1 on page 66, trim the quilted pieces to the appropriate size and shape. Cut two pieces from the lining, noting the different cutting lines on the pattern.

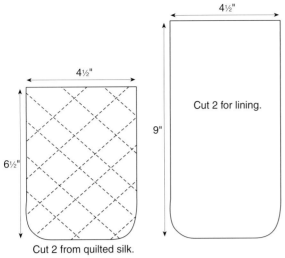

Fig. 1
Cut eyeglasses case pieces.

Step 8. With right sides together, pin the quilted pieces together and stitch ¼ inch from the long and curved edges. Pink the curved area to notch out the fullness. Press the seams open over a point presser, finger-pressing the curved area if necessary. Turn right side out.

Step 9. Repeat with the lining pieces, leaving a ⅝-inch-long opening as shown (Fig. 2) for the drawstring on one side.

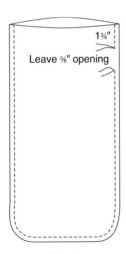

Fig. 2
Sew lining pieces together.

Step 10. Slip the quilted case inside the lining with right sides together, seams matching and the upper raw edges even. Stitch ¼ inch from the raw edges, leaving a 3-inch-long opening for turning. Press the seam open and trim the seam allowances at the side seams to reduce bulk.

Step 11. Turn right side out through the opening and

slipstitch the opening closed. Tuck the lining inside, allowing for a 1¼-inch-wide band of the lining to show at the upper edge.

Step 12. Turn the case so the lining side is out and hand-tack the lining to the lower corners of the batting at the bottom edge. Turn right side out.

Step 13.
Topstitch ½ and ⅞ inch from the upper edge of the lining band (Fig. 3).

Step 14. Use a tapestry needle to feed the rattail cord through the opening. Add a drop of seam

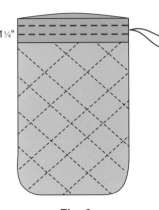

Fig. 3
Topstitch band and thread cord through casing.

sealant to each end of the cord and allow to dry.

Step 15. Slip two or three beads onto each end of the cord and knot the cord ends to keep the beads in place. Tuck your glasses inside and you're good to go!

Instructions
Pieced Case

Project Note: *Use ¼-inch-wide seam allowances. Press cotton batting flat.*

Step 1. Cut five 1½-inch-wide bias strips from each fabric. They will range from 2–15 inches long.

Step 2. Position a short strip of Fabric A diagonally across one corner of the batting square. With right sides together, position a strip of Fabric B on top of Fabric A and pin in place. Stitch. Flip strip B onto the batting and press. Add a strip of Fabric C in the same manner. Stitch, flip and press (Fig. 4).

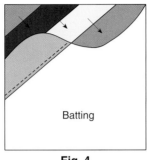

Batting

Fig. 4
Press in direction of arrows.

Step 3. Repeat Step 2 until the entire piece of batting is covered with fabric strips. Trim the excess strips even with the batting edges.

Step 4. Referring to Fig. 5, make a pattern for the case on pattern tracing cloth or tissue and cut out. Cut one from the pieced fabric and one from the lining.

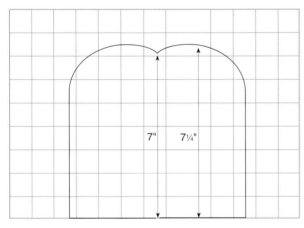

7"   7¼"

Fig. 5
Make pattern.
1 square = 1"

Step 5. With right sides together, pin the upper curved edges of the pieced case and the lining together. Measure 5¾ inches from the lower edge on each side and mark with a pin. Stitch the curved edges together from pin to pin, backstitching at the beginning and end of the stitching. Cut a small notch in the seam allowance at the end of the stitching on both long raw edges. Clip the upper inward curve (Fig. 6).

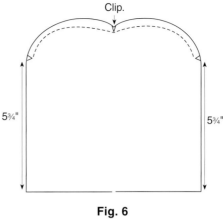

Clip.

5¾"   5¾"

Fig. 6
Sew lining to pieced case.

Step 6. Open the lining piece out of the way of the outer case. With right sides together, stitch ¼ inch from the raw edges, pivoting slightly at the notch (Fig. 7). Stitch across the short end of the outer case and clip the corners. Repeat with the short end of the lining, leaving a 2-inch-long opening.

Step 7. Turn the case right side out through the opening in the lining. Turn in the opening edges and machine stitch them together.

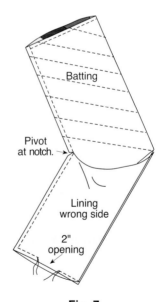

Batting

Pivot at notch.

Lining wrong side

2" opening

Fig. 7
Stitch long edges of case and lining together.

Step 8. Tuck the lining into the eyeglasses cover, then turn the case lining side out and tack the lining to the batting at both corners. Turn right side out and press as needed. ❖

Veggie Lover's Handbag

When you create your own version of this humorous handbag, you can carry your favorite veggie with you all summer long. A plastic carrot from the floral department of your local craft store makes a great handle. If you don't like carrots, substitute plastic celery, asparagus spears, green onions or string beans for the handle. Add a photo-transfer border like the bunnies shown for added conversational value, and be ready for amused glances from admiring onlookers.

DESIGN BY LUCY B. GRAY

Project Specifications
Size: 4 x 8½ x 10 inches

Materials
Project Notes: *Choose the handle for your bag first and then select fabrics in colors and themes that complement the handle. Choose prints with different design scales to play off each other.*

If fabrics are not medium weight, you will need to reinforce them with an additional layer of lightweight fusible interfacing or muslin underlining as instructed in the directions that follow.

- ½ yard medium-weight print for bag
- ½ yard medium-weight coordinating print for lining and upper-edge binding
- 12 x 16-inch garment-weight leather or imitation suede (or a leather skirt from a thrift store)
- ¾ yard of 44/45-inch-wide muslin
- ⅓ yard polyester fleece
- Plastic carrot approximately 10 inches long from the tip of the carrot to the end of the leaves
- Paper-backed fusible web
- Ruler and marking pen
- Pattern tracing cloth or tissue
- Spray-on craft adhesive
- Spray-on fabric protector
- Rubber mallet (or hammer with padded peen) and pliers
- Glue stick
- Bull-nose binder clips (for holding leather layers together for stitching)
- Teflon presser foot
- #14 leather sewing machine needle
- Fast-drying fabric glue
- 1 sheet plastic canvas
- 3 (⅝-inch-diameter) buttons

- 1 (1-inch-diameter) button
- Fabric tube turner
- 2 magnetic snaps
- 4 x 4-inch piece of plastic cut from a clean milk jug
- Permanent marking pen
- Craft knife or razor blade
- Electric drill and $\frac{3}{16}$-inch-diameter drill bit
- Leather hand-sewing needle (#5 or larger)
- Computer with photo-editing software and ink-jet printer (optional)
- 1 sheet of ink-jet transfer paper (optional)
- Photocopies of clipart design images (optional)

Instructions

Step 1. Preshrink the muslin, bag and lining fabrics. Press to remove wrinkles.

Step 2. Enlarge the pattern in Fig. 1 on pattern tracing cloth or tissue, and cut out.

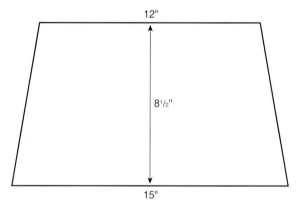

12"

8½"

15"

Fig. 1
Make pattern.

Step 3. Use the pattern to cut two bag pieces, two bag-lining pieces and four muslin pieces. Serge or machine baste a muslin piece to the wrong side of each bag and lining piece for added stability. Also cut two bag pieces from fleece.

Step 4. One at a time, apply a coat of spray adhesive to one side of both pieces of the polyester fleece. Place each piece of fleece with sprayed side down on the wrong side of a bag piece. Weight the pieces with heavy books for several minutes to ensure maximum adhesion. Before the adhesive is completely dry, lift the edges of the fleece so you can trim away ½ inch at the side and bottom edges to eliminate bulk in the seams.

Step 5. Apply several coats of spray-on fabric protector to the right side of each fleece-backed

bag piece and to the right side of the lining pieces. Allow to dry.

Step 6. If desired, apply heat-transfer images to the lower edge of each bag panel. Be sure to arrange them between the seam allowances and 1–1½ inches or more above the lower edge so that you don't stitch into them. See sidebar on page 73 for how-tos.

Step 7. For the bag bottom, cut two 3½ x 16-inch pieces from the leather or imitation suede. With right sides together, position one leather strip so that one long edge lies ¾ inch from the lower edge of the bag piece. Use glue stick in the ¼-inch-wide seam allowance of the leather to hold it in place. Insert a #14 leather sewing machine needle and lengthen the stitch. Attach the Teflon presser foot to make sewing easier. Stitch ¼ inch from the leather edge (Fig. 2). Turn the leather panel down over the bag lower edge and finger-press along the seam edge or use the rubber mallet to flatten the seam. Trim the short ends of the leather strips even with the side edges of the bag panels, continuing the angle as shown in Fig. 3. Repeat for the other bag piece.

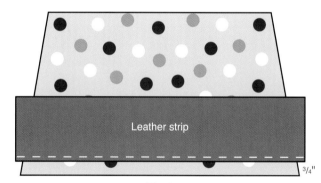

Leather strip

¾"

Fig. 2
Sew leather strip to lower edges of bag pieces.

Fig. 3
Trim excess leather.

Step 8. With right sides facing, pin the bag panels together. Use binder clips to hold the leather edges together. Stitch ½ inch from the side edges of the bag and ¼ inch from the lower edge of the bag. Finger-press the seams open and secure them with dots of fast-drying fabric glue.

Step 9. To create boxed corners, align the side seam with the bottom seam at one bottom corner and pound the resulting triangle flat using the rubber mallet. With a ruler, draw a line perpendicular to the side seam 2 inches from the point (Fig. 4). Clip the layers together and stitch on the line. Trim the point, leaving a ½-inch-wide seam allowance Repeat for the other corner. Turn the bag right side out and use your fingers to manipulate the corners so they are true and the bag sits squarely on a flat surface.

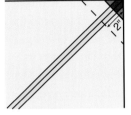

Fig. 4
Align side and bottom seams.
Stitch 2" from point.

Step 10. Cut a piece of plastic canvas slightly smaller than the inside of the bag bottom and place inside the bag. Working with one corner at a time, squirt a large blob of fast-drying glue through the mesh to the fleece beneath. Finger-press the plastic into the glue and hold it there while the glue sets.

Step 11. If desired, machine quilt a diagonal grid pattern on the lining pieces to add more body. Cut and make pockets of the desired size and shape, and sew them to the right side of the lining pieces. Check out the pockets in your favorite handbags to use as inspiration.

Step 12. Using a generous ⅝-inch-wide side seam allowance and following Steps 8 and 9 above, sew the bag-lining pieces together and box the bottom corners as you did for the bag. Do not turn the lining right side out. Tuck it into the bag and check the fit. If it is too large, stitch deeper side and bottom seams. When the lining fits smoothly inside the bag without wrinkles or excess fullness, remove it from the bag and set it aside.

Step 13. To finish the bag's upper edge, cut enough 2½-inch-wide strips on the true bias from the lining fabric to make a 30-inch-long strip of binding. Sew the

strips together using bias seams and press them open. Apply several coats of spray-on fabric protector to the binding and allow to dry. Fold under ½ inch on one short end of the binding and press.

Step 14. Beginning with the folded end about an inch from the lining's side seam, pin the binding even with the lining top edge, right sides together. Allow a 1-inch overlap where the binding ends meet, then trim the excess. Stitch the binding to the lining with a ⅝-inch-wide seam allowance. Set the lining aside while you prepare the handle with straps.

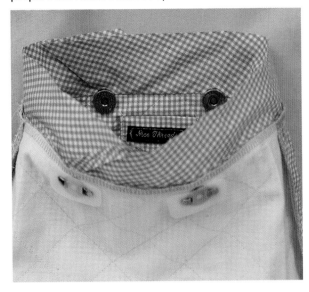

Step 15. Refer to the how-to photos on page 72 for steps 15 and 16. Using a ³⁄₁₆-inch drill bit, drill through the carrot about an inch from each end (Photo A).

Step 16. To make the fabric straps for the handle shanks, cut two 1½ x 24-inch strips from the bag fabric. Fold the strips in half, right sides together, and stitch ⅜ inch from the raw edges. Turn them right side out with a tube turner and press flat. Thread one end of one strap through one of the holes in the carrot and pull half of it through the hole (Photo B). To tie the strap securely to the carrot, crisscross the strap ends over the top of the carrot above the holes, then wrap them around the body of the carrot so that the holes are covered, and, finally, tie them in a tight square knot directly underneath (Photo C). Tie seven more tight square knots on top of the first knot, creating a stiff, 1½-inch-long shank for the handle. Tie a final half knot in each strip, about 1½ inches below the square knots, and trim (Photo D). Repeat with the remaining fabric strap at the other end of the carrot.

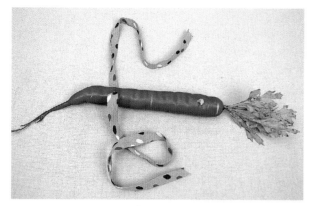

Photo A

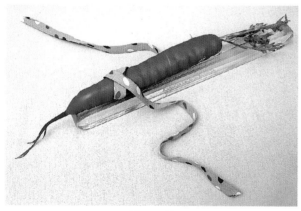

Photo B

Photo C

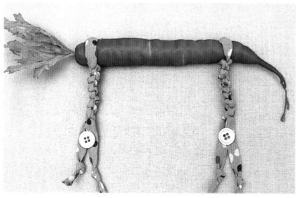

Photo D

Step 17. Center the knotted handle shanks inside against the *back* bag lining so that they lie equidistant from the bag sides, and the horizontal carrot handle is 1½ inches above the lining upper edge. Pin in place temporarily. Place the perforated metal disks from the magnetic snap set between the shanks on the lining/binding seam line. With a marking pen, lightly draw two lines where the snap prongs must pierce the fabric. Cut these marks cleanly with a craft knife or razor blade.

Step 18. Cut sturdy snap reinforcements from the piece of milk-jug plastic, making them slightly larger than the perforated metal disks. Poke the female snap prongs through the slits in the lining and anchor them on the back of the lining with the punch-out pieces. Next, add the plastic pieces and bend the prongs outward over them for added strength. Make the prongs lie as flat as possible with pliers or a padded hammer so the snaps don't pull away from the fabric later. Collapse the lining and press the front inside binding firmly against the female snaps on the back binding to imprint the location for the male halves of the snaps. Place the perforated metal disks on the imprints, and mark where to slit the fabric for the prongs. Install the male snap parts over the lining seam line.

Step 19. Referring to Photo E below, anchor the handle shanks securely to the lining by positioning a ⅝-inch button on top of the strap ends just below the last square knot in the series. Sew through the button and fabric layers using matching thread. Then sew the knotted shanks securely along both sides to the lining.

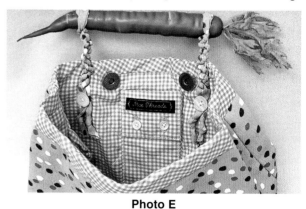

Photo E

Step 20. Place the lining inside the outer shell for the last time with the upper raw edges even and the side seams matching. Tuck the carrot handle and the binding strip down into the bag and out of the way. Serge or zigzag the upper edges of the bag and lining together.

Step 21. Flip the binding up and then down over the upper edge to the outside of the bag. Turn under the raw edge so the binding is 1 inch wide and slipstitch in place.

Step 22. For additional embellishment, stack a small button on top of a large button at the center on the bag front. Sew in place. ❖

Transfer It

If you are computer savvy, you can create a complementary decorative border for your bag using photo-editing software and heat-transfer images generated by your ink-jet printer. For this bag, I scanned 18th-century rabbit and carrot images from the Dover Clip-Art Series and the Dover Pictorial Archives and manipulated them with Adobe Photoshop before transferring them to plain fabric using ink-jet transfer paper.

Transfer papers are available in craft and fabric stores. I used Ink-jet 2T Paper by WPI. If you've never done something like this, test the technique on fabric scraps before attempting it on your bag fabric.

1. Test your design layout first by scanning or photocopying your images, cutting them out and arranging them along the lower edge of the bag pattern, inside the seam lines. Adjust the image sizes to create a lively, interesting arrangement.

2. When you're satisfied with your design, import your images into your computer's photo-editing program and save this picture file with the same dimensions as your bag pattern.

3. Next, create a new blank picture file that is 8½ x 11 inches (the size of the ink-jet transfer paper). Go back to your first file and cut it up at strategic places so that all the pieces can fit on a single transfer sheet. Move the cut pieces from the original file to the new picture file, arranging them so they all fit on the page. If you can, include a few extra images to experiment with on scrap fabric or prepare a second sheet with additional transfers to test.

4. Next, reverse the images and colorize them with the software to complement the bag fabric (I had visions of purple rabbits munching away in my garden). Following the transfer manufacturer's directions, print this new picture file onto a sheet of ink-jet transfer paper. Allow the ink to dry thoroughly.

5. Following the transfer manufacturer's directions, transfer an image or two to white or off-white fabric scraps to test the technique. When you are comfortable with the process, arrange the images for each half of the bag and transfer to white muslin. Leave the paper cover sheet in place.

6. Apply a piece of paper-backed fusible web to the wrong side of each transfer-fabric section, following the manufacturer's directions. Allow to cool completely.

7. Remove the fusible backing paper and the transfer cover paper. Cut out the images and place them in position, right side up, on the bag fabric. Cover them with the paper backing (shiny side down, facing the transfer), and iron firmly in place with a dry iron. If the transfer peels up as you lift the paper backing, press the paper back down over the transfer and reheat it with the iron. This step takes a bit of finesse, gently heating and pressing until everything is securely bonded in place.

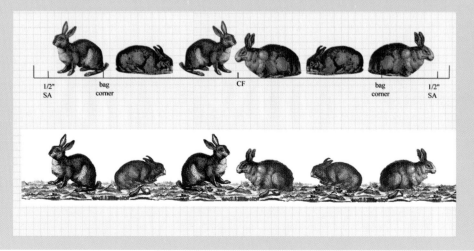

Shell Seekers Porch Set

Bring the fresh ocean breezes to your porch or patio with these seaworthy, shell-inspired pieces for your porch or patio.

DESIGNS BY JANE SCHENCK

Project Specifications

Place Mats: 13 x 19 inches

Napkins: 21 inches square

Chair Cushions: 16 x 17 inches (customize to your chair)

Starfish Pillow: 16 inches, point to point

Conch Pillow: 16 x 9½ inches

Scallop Pillow: 11½ x 14 inches

Materials
Two Place Mats, Napkins & Napkin Rings

- 1¾ yards 44/45-inch-wide sand-colored solid (medium weight)
- 4 yards narrow cord for piping
- Peach, tan, and dark orange cotton print scraps for appliqués
- 12 x 28-inch piece coordinating print for piping and napkin rings
- 2 yards ⅜-inch-diameter cord to cover for napkin rings

Two Chair Cushions

- 1 yard 54-inch-wide home decor fabric
- 2 yards decorative cord for ties
- Liquid seam sealant

Pillows (one each)

Project Note: *Yardages are given for 44/45-inch-wide cotton.*

- ⅝ yard light brown or peach tone-on-tone print for starfish
- ½ yard dark red tone-on-tone print for scallop and conch shells
- ⅓ yard peach tone-on-tone print or solid-color fabric for conch shell

All Projects

- All-purpose thread in colors to match fabrics
- Pattern tracing cloth or tissue
- Air- or water-soluble marking pen
- 3 yards polyester fleece for cushions, place mats and pillows
- 20-ounce bag polyester fiberfill for pillow stuffing
- ¼ yard paper-backed fusible web
- ½ yard tear-away stabilizer

Instructions
Two Place Mats, Napkins &
Napkin Rings

Step 1. From the sand-colored fabric, cut four rectangles each 14 x 20 inches for placemats. Cut two from fleece. For the napkins, cut two 21¾-inch squares from the sand-colored fabric. From the coordinating fabric, cut a 24-inch square. Cut 1½-inch-wide bias strips and join with bias seams to make one long strip, or cut continuous bias following the directions in the sidebar on page 79.

Step 2. For the appliqués, trace two each of the shell templates for place mats and napkins on pages 78 and 89 onto the paper side of fusible web. Cut out matching shapes in groups of two. Fuse the pieces to the wrong side of appropriately colored scraps. Cut out the shapes. Remove the backing paper.

Step 3. Make narrow, double hems at all edges of the napkin squares. Position a small scallop shell in one corner of each napkin square with the bottom edge about 1⅝ inches from the corner.

Step 4. Use the edge of a dessert plate or other rounded shape to draw curved edges at each corner of each place-mat rectangle. Cut on the lines. Position the large shell appliqués in identical sets along the left-hand edge on the right side of two place mats. Fuse in place following manufacturer's directions. Pin tear-away stabilizer in place behind each appliqué. Adjust the machine for a narrow satin stitch. Stitch the detail lines in each shell and then stitch over the appliqué raw edges. Remove the stabilizer.

Step 5. Position each appliquéd piece face up on a piece of fleece and pin the layers together. Machine baste ½ inch from the raw edges.

Step 6. Wrap the continuous strip of bias around the narrow cord for piping with the right side out and cut edges even. Using a zipper foot, stitch close to the cord (Fig. 1). Trim the seam allowances to a scant ¼ inch.

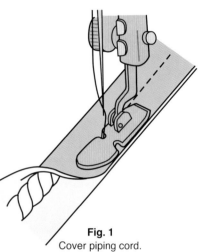

Fig. 1
Cover piping cord.

Step 7. With the cord just beyond the basting toward the place-mat center, pin piping to each place mat. Clip the seam allowance as needed to ease it around the corners; allow for a 1-inch overlap at the starting and ending point on one long edge of the place mat. Using a zipper or cording foot, sew the piping in place, beginning and ending the stitching 1 inch from each end of the piping. To finish the piping, remove the piping stitching in the unstitched ends. On one end, cut off the filler cord so that both cut ends meet. Turn the fabric under ⅜ inch and press on one end. Wrap the turned edge over the raw edges and stitch the remainder of the piping in place (Fig 2).

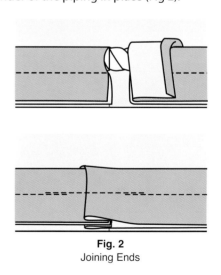

Fig. 2
Joining Ends

Step 8. With right sides together, pin the place-mat backs to the place-mat fronts. Stitch from the wrong side of the mat fronts so you can see the piping stitching. Stitch just inside the first stitching. It may feel like you are *crowding* the piping cord as you stitch. Turn the place mat right side out and press. Slipstitch the opening closed.

Step 9. With right sides together, encase 1 yard of the 2 yards of ⅜-inch cord in a 1-yard-long bias strip of coordinating fabric (Fig. 3). Do not cut away the excess cord. Using a zipper foot to stitch close to the cord, stitch across the short end of the bias and the cord, and then pivot and continue stitching to the end of the bias and the cord. Be careful not to catch the cord in the stitching. Trim the seams to a scant ¼ inch. To turn the bias onto the uncovered section of cord, pull on the end of the encased cord and push the fabric along the cord and onto the uncovered cord. Cut across the stitched short end to eliminate the uncovered cord. Discard the uncovered cord or save for another project.

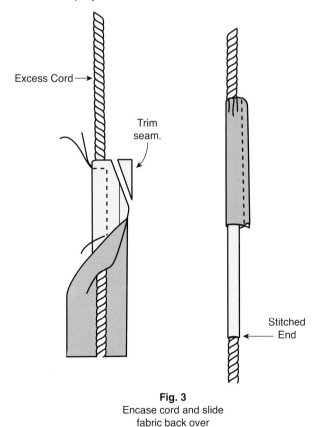

Excess Cord →

Trim seam.

Stitched End ←

Fig. 3
Encase cord and slide
fabric back over
the excess.

Step 10. To make each napkin ring, wrap and pin the encased cord around a 1½-inch-diameter spool of thread. Slide the cord ring off the spool and tuck the raw ends inside the ring. Working on the inside of the ring, whipstitch the edges of the cord together.

Chair Cushions

Project Note: *Before cutting, measure the seat of the chair to be cushioned. If needed, adjust the pattern to customize the fit.*

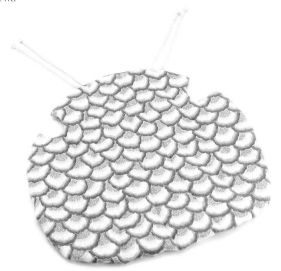

Step 1. Enlarge the chair-cushion patterns (Fig. 4 see page 80) on pattern cloth or tissue and cut out. From the decorator print, cut four seat cushions. Cut six from fleece.

Step 2. For each cushion, place three layers of fleece on a flat surface with one print piece right side up on top. Machine baste ½ inch from the raw edges.

Step 3. With right sides together, pin a second print piece to print-fleece unit. Leaving an opening along the bottom edge, stitch the layers together ½ inch from the raw edges. Turn right side out and slipstitch the opening closed.

Step 4. Place the cushions, padded side up, on a flat surface and use straight pins through all layers to mark quilting lines. Pins should point toward the base of the shell (not the outer curved edge).

Step 5. Lengthen the stitch or use a special built-in quilting stitch if available. Machine stitch on the lines, removing pins as you reach them and stitching from the base of the shell shape to the outer curved edge. Stitch off the edge. Do not backstitch. Pull the threads to the underside and tie off or thread into a hand-sewing needle and bury in the cushion layers.

Step 6. Cut four 18-inch-long pieces of decorative cord and tie a knot at each end. Apply seam sealant to the cut ends. Fold the cords in half and hand tack the center of each cord to the back of the cushion, customizing the cord placement to the chair as needed so you can tie the cushions in place.

Pillows

Step 1. From the peach or brown print for the starfish, cut two stars. Cut two from fleece. From the red for the scallop, cut two shells. Cut two from fleece. Also cut one conch shell inset and two from fleece. From the peach for the conch shell, cut one pillow top and one pillow back. Cut one each from fleece.

Step 2. For each pillow shape, place its fleece layers on a flat surface with the fabric shape on top, right side up. Baste the layers together. Mark the quilting lines on the pillow tops using an air- or water-soluble marking pen. Stitch the layers together on the marked lines.

Step 3. For the conch pillow, sew the red pillow top piece to the peach pillow piece along the curved edge. Stitch ½ inch from the raw edges and press the seam toward the peach piece. *Do not trim the seam.* Hand

sew the seam allowances to the fleece underneath to build up a slight edge between the parts of the shell.

Step 4. For added dimension in the stitched rings of the conch shell, carefully make a slit in the back layer of fleece in each ring area and add fiberfill stuffing (Fig. 5). Catchstitch the slit edges together to contain the fiberfill.

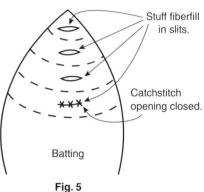

Fig. 5
Slash batting and
add stuffing in
stitched areas.

Step 5. With right sides together, stitch the pillow fronts to the matching pillow backs, leaving an opening for turning. Turn the pillows right side out.

Step 6. Stuff each pillow with fiberfill to the desired firmness and slipstitch the openings closed. ❖

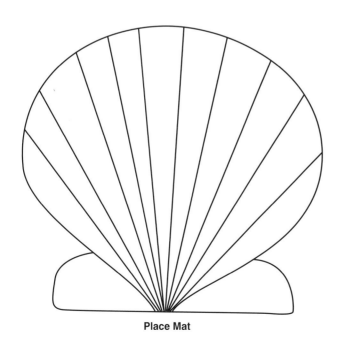

Place Mat

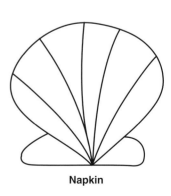

Napkin

TEMPLATES CONTINUED ON PAGE 89

Make It Quick!

To make a strip of continuous bias:

1. Cut the 24-inch square in half diagonally and sew together (Fig. 6) using a ¼-inch-wide seam allowance. Press the seam open.

2. On the wrong side of the fabric and working from bias edge to bias edge, measure and mark 1½-inch-wide strip segments. Trim off any excess beyond the last line. Number the diagonal lines as shown (Fig. 7).

3. With right sides together, match the bias edges so that the numbers are offset as shown in Fig. 8 and there is a tail of fabric at each end of the seam. Stitch together ¼ inch from the raw edges. Cut along the lines for a continuous strip of bias.

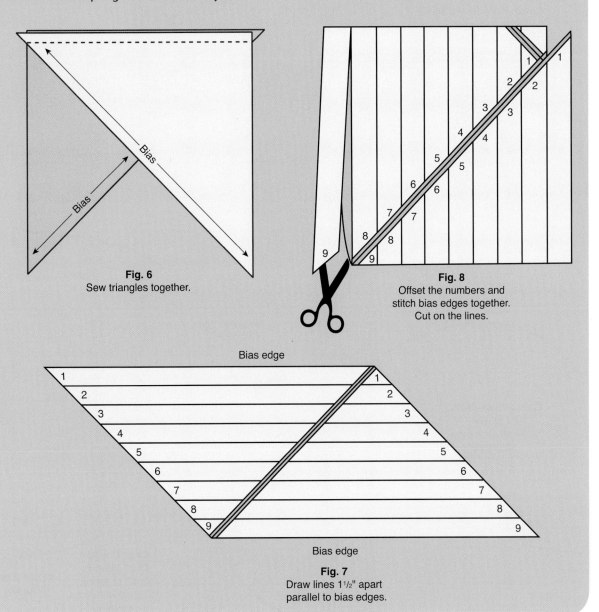

Fig. 6
Sew triangles together.

Fig. 8
Offset the numbers and
stitch bias edges together.
Cut on the lines.

Fig. 7
Draw lines 1½" apart
parallel to bias edges.

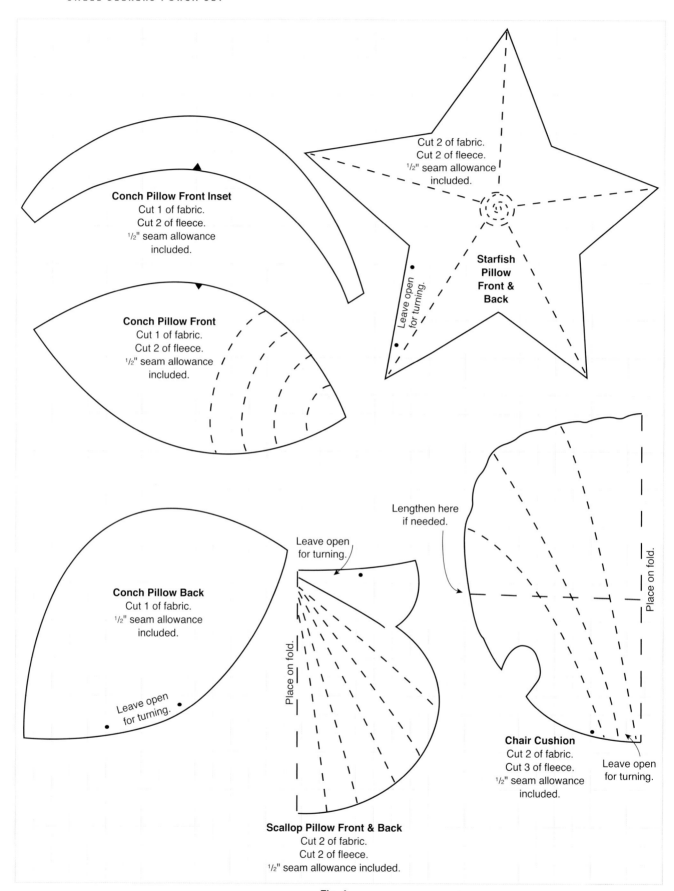

Conch Pillow Front Inset
Cut 1 of fabric.
Cut 2 of fleece.
$1/2$" seam allowance
included.

Cut 2 of fabric.
Cut 2 of fleece.
$1/2$" seam allowance
included.

**Starfish
Pillow
Front &
Back**

Leave open
for turning.

Conch Pillow Front
Cut 1 of fabric.
Cut 2 of fleece.
$1/2$" seam allowance
included.

Conch Pillow Back
Cut 1 of fabric.
$1/2$" seam allowance
included.

Leave open
for turning.

Leave open
for turning.

Lengthen here
if needed.

Place on fold.

Place on fold.

Chair Cushion
Cut 2 of fabric.
Cut 3 of fleece.
$1/2$" seam allowance
included.

Leave open
for turning.

Scallop Pillow Front & Back
Cut 2 of fabric.
Cut 2 of fleece.
$1/2$" seam allowance included.

Fig. 4
Scale: 1 square = 1"

Green Thumb
Gardening Apron

This apron offers a pretty yet practical approach to dressing for your outdoor passion. Five lined pockets keep your tools handy.

DESIGN BY PAM ARCHER

Project Specifications
Apron Size: One size fits all

Materials
- 1 yard firmly woven cotton canvas or duck for apron and pocket linings
- ½ yard coordinating floral print for pockets
- ⅓ yard coordinating plaid for binding
- ¼ yard lightweight nonwoven fusible interfacing
- All-purpose thread to match fabrics
- Rotary cutter, mat and ruler
- Pattern tracing cloth or tissue
- Basic sewing tools and equipment

Instructions
Step 1. Enlarge the apron and side pocket patterns on page 83 on pattern tracing cloth or tissue and cut out.

Step 2. From the canvas, cut one apron and two side pockets. For the waistband, cut one strip 2¼ x 28 inches. For the ties, cut two strips each 2¼ x 19¼ inches. Cut one 8¼ x 19-inch strip for back of the center pocket.

Step 3. From the coordinating floral, cut two side pockets and one 8¼ x 19-inch rectangle for the center pocket.

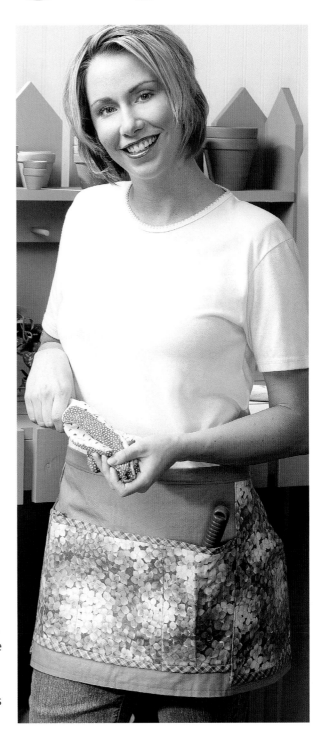

Step 4. From the coordinating plaid, cut enough 1¾-inch-wide bias strips to make a continuous strip 75 inches long.

Step 5. From the interfacing, cut two strips each 2¼ x 19¼ inches and one strip 2¼ x 28 inches.

Step 6. Serge- or zigzag-finish the side and lower edges of the apron panel. Turn under and press a ½-inch-wide hem at the lower side edges and then the upper angled side edge. Stitch ⅜ inch from the folded edges. Repeat at the apron lower edges. Form tucks at the upper edge of the apron with the folded edges toward the side edges. Pin in place and then machine baste ½ inch from the raw edges (Fig. 1).

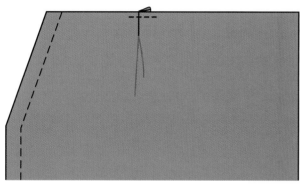

Fig. 1
Make tucks at upper edge of apron.

Step 7. With wrong sides facing and raw edges even, pin the canvas and floral center-pocket rectangles together. Machine baste ¼ inch from all raw edges. Serge- or zigzag-finish the short edges of the layered pocket panel.

Step 8. With the flower side of the pocket panel face up, make two tucks at the lower edge as shown in Fig. 2. Pin in place and baste ¼ inch from the raw edges across each tuck. Fold the tucks in place at the upper edge of the pocket panel and pin in place temporarily.

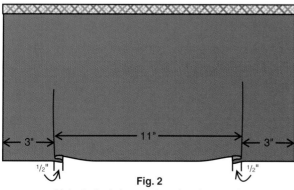

Fig. 2
Make tucks in lower edge of pocket panel.

Step 9. Using bias seams, sew the bias strips together to make one long strip. Press the seams open. Serge- or zigzag-finish one long edge of the strip.

Step 10. From the bias strip, cut one 19-inch-long piece. With right sides together and raw edges even, pin and stitch the bias to the upper edge of the center pocket panel. Use a ⅜-inch-wide seam allowance. Press the bias toward the seam allowance and then wrap it over the seam edge to enclose it in the bias. From the right side, stitch in the ditch of the seam, catching the underside of the bias in the stitching (Fig. 3). Apply bias to the lower edge of the pocket panel in the same manner.

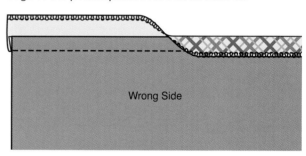

Fig. 3
Stitch binding to pocket edges.

Step 11. Position the center pocket on the right side of the apron panel with centers matching and the lower edge of the pocket 1½ inches above the lower edge. Stitch in place, stitching in the ditch of the binding seam at the pocket's lower edge. Topstitch the pocket to the apron 3 inches from the center front on each half of the pocket (Fig. 4). Machine baste the short ends of the center pocket to the apron.

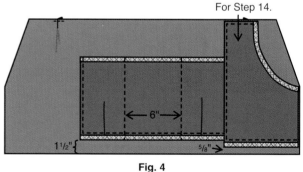

Fig. 4
Sew center pocket to apron.

Step 12. Trim ⅛ inch from the longest edge of each canvas side pocket. With right sides together, pin a canvas side pocket to each floral-print side pocket along the long and short side edges. Because you trimmed the canvas, the pocket will "bow" slightly. Stitch ⅝ inch from the long and short side edges. Trim the seam allowances to ¼ inch and turn the pockets right side out. Press, allowing the canvas to roll to the underside at both edges so it doesn't show. Machine baste the pocket layers together ¼ inch from the remaining raw edges.

Step 13. For each pocket, cut a 10½-inch-long piece from the bias strip. With right sides together and raw edges even, pin a bias strip to the upper curved edge of each pocket. Allow the excess bias to extend beyond the pocket side edge. Stitch ⅝ inch from the raw edges and trim the seam allowance to ⅜ inch. Press the bias toward the seam and wrap it to the underside of the pocket, turning the raw edge in at the lower edge of the curve (trim excess to ¼ inch). Pin in place and stitch in the ditch from the pocket right side. Finish the lower edge of each pocket in the same manner, using a 9-inch-long piece of bias for each one and allowing for ¼ inch of bias extending at each side edge of the pocket. Trim the excess.

Step 14. Position the side pockets on the apron panel with the inside finished edges ⅝ inch in from the raw edges of the center pocket panel and the lower finished edge ⅝ inch above the lower edge of the apron. Pin in place. Topstitch ¼ inch from both finished edges of the pocket. Stitch in the ditch of the binding seam at the lower edge of each pocket.

Step 15. Apply fusible interfacing to the wrong side of each strip for the waistband and ties. With right sides together and using a ⅝-inch-wide seam, sew each tie to a short end of the waistband. Trim the seams to ¼ inch and press the seams open. Turn under and press ⅝ inch on one long edge of the strip. Trim to ⅜ inch.

Step 16. With right sides together and centers matching, pin the raw edge of the waistband to the upper edge of the apron. Stitch ⅝ inch from the raw edges and press the waistband toward the seam. Turn under and press ⅝ inch at the long edges of the tie. Trim the seam allowances to ⅜ inch.

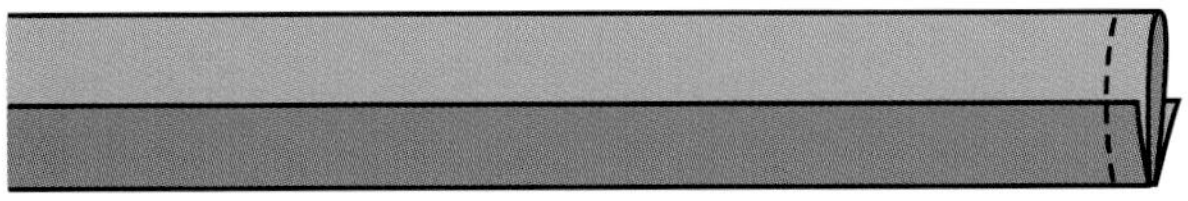

Fig. 5
Fold and stitch 1/4" from tie ends.

Step 17. Fold the tie ends in half with right sides together and stitch ¼ inch from the short raw edges (Fig.5). Clip the corners and turn right side out. Pin the long folded edges of the tie together, continuing along the waistband inner edge. Topstitch ¼ inch from the folded edges, continuing along the waistband and then to the end of the other tie.

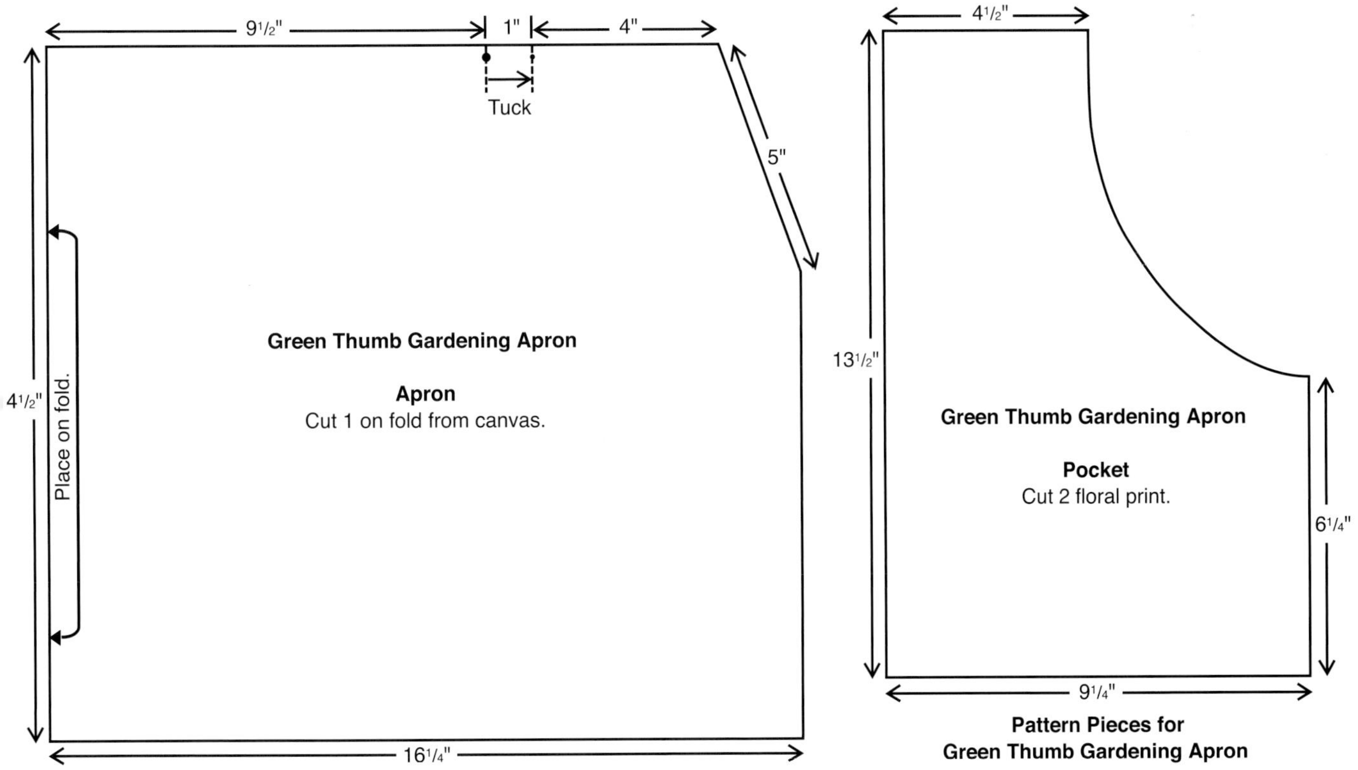
9 1/2"
1"
4"
Tuck
5"
4 1/2"
Place on fold.
Green Thumb Gardening Apron
Apron
Cut 1 on fold from canvas.
16 1/4"
4 1/2"
13 1/2"
Green Thumb Gardening Apron
Pocket
Cut 2 floral print.
6 1/4"
9 1/4"

Pattern Pieces for Green Thumb Gardening Apron

Kissy Fish Lap Quilt

A clever twist of color placement turns the traditional Hunter's Star block into colorful tropical fish, rubbing noses in their watery background. It is a wonderful lap quilt or the perfect wall hanging for creating a focal point in a child's room.

DESIGN BY MEG TRYBA

Project Specifications

Quilt Size: 54½ inches square

Materials

Project Note: All yardages are for 44/45-inch-wide cotton.

- ¾ yard aqua tone-on-tone print for water background color
- 1 yard yellow tone-on-tone print for fish bodies and the inner and middle borders
- ⅓ yard red print for fish noses and middle border
- ⅓ yard green print for fish noses and middle border
- ¼ yard orange print for fish tails
- ¼ yard teal tone-on-tone print for fish tails
- ⅝ yard dark blue tone-on-tone print for the star points
- ⅝ yard dark blue tone-on-tone print for middle border
- 2 yards fish print for the outer border and binding
- 3¼ yards coordinating print for backing
- 60-inch square of batting
- 6-inch-square rotary-cutting ruler
- Rotary cutter and mat
- All-purpose thread to match fabrics
- Basic sewing tools and equipment
- Crystals and applicator for fish eyes (optional)

Instructions

Project Notes: Preshrink all fabrics and press to remove wrinkles. Strip cutting is based on a usable width of 42 inches after preshrinking. All seam allowances are ¼ inch wide unless otherwise noted.

Step 1. From the aqua print, cut eight 10-inch squares. Cut the squares in half twice diagonally for 32 quarter-square triangles. From the yellow tone-on-tone print, cut four strips each 2 x 42 inches for inner border and eight strips each 2¼ x 42 inches wide for the fish bodies. From the red print, cut four strips each 1¾ x 42 inches. From the green print, cut four strips each 1¾ x 42 inches. From the orange print, cut three strips each 2 x 42 inches; crosscut a total of 16 pieces each 2 x 6 inches. From the teal tone-on-tone print, cut three strips each 2 x 42 inches; crosscut a total of 16 pieces each 2 x 6 inches. From the dark blue tone-on-tone print for the star points, cut eight strips each 2 x 42 inches wide; crosscut 64 pieces each 2 x 4½ inches.

Step 2. From the dark blue print for the pieced middle border, cut four strips each 3½ x 42 inches. From two of the strips, cut a total of eight pieces each 3½ x 10 inches. From the fish print for the outer border and binding, cut four border strips each 6 inches wide, cutting along

Make It Yours

The Traditional Hunter's Star block looks like this. Notice how color placement plays a role in determining the final effect. Play with colors to make your own new version of this classic design.

the length of the yardage. For the binding, cut four lengthwise strips each 2¾ inches wide.

Step 3. Sew each of four 2¼-inch yellow tone-on-tone strips to a 1¾-inch green strip and press toward the green strip. Repeat with the remaining yellow strips and the red strips. You should have a total of eight strip units for the fish.

Step 4. Cut triangles from the strip units, placing the point of the ruler on the red or green strip as shown (Fig. 1). Align the edge of the body strip with the 5-inch marks on the ruler. Make the first cut to create a 45-degree angle and discard the selvage edge pieces. Cut along the adjacent edge of the ruler to create a nose-unit triangle. Carefully rotate the ruler to the other side of the strip set, and cut a second triangle. Set aside this and all other triangles cut from this edge of the strip unit for the pieced middle border. Continue rotating the ruler and cutting triangles from both sides of the strip unit. You will need 16 nose units

and 12 border units from the red/yellow and the same number from the green/yellow strip sets. Mark the center of the long edge of each of the nose units (Figs. 2).

Step 5. Cut triangles in this same manner from the 3½ x 42-inch dark blue print strips for the pieced middle border. You will need a total of 20 dark blue print triangles. Set all triangles aside.

Step 6. Divide the 2 x 4½-inch dark blue tone-on-tone rectangles into two stacks of 32 each. On the wrong side of a rectangle, draw a 45-degree line from one corner to the opposite long edge as shown in Fig. 3. Mark 32 in this manner. On the rectangles in the second stack, draw the line from the opposite corner.

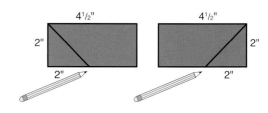

Fig. 3
Mark rectangles.

Step 7. Mark the center of one long edge on each 2 x 6-inch orange and each 2 x 6-inch teal rectangle. Place a marked blue rectangle face down at the right-hand end of each orange rectangle. Stitch on the line and trim the seam to ¼ inch. Press the seam toward the dark blue. Add a dark blue rectangle to the opposite end of the orange rectangle in the same fashion. Make 16 units. Repeat with the remaining blue rectangles

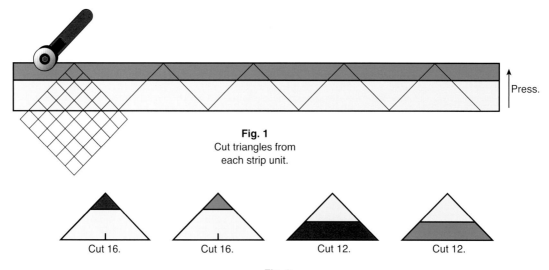

Fig. 1
Cut triangles from
each strip unit.

Cut 16.   Cut 16.   Cut 12.   Cut 12.

Fig. 2
Mark center of each nose unit.

and the teal rectangles for a total of 32 fish tails, 16 of each color combination (Fig. 4).

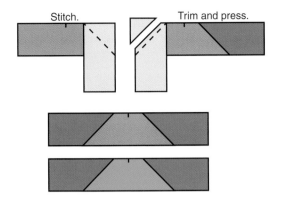

Stitch.   Trim and press.

Fig. 4
Make fish-tail units.

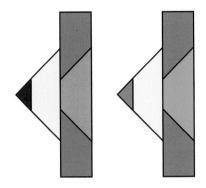

Fig. 5
Sew fish tails to nose units.
Make 16 of each.

Step 8. With center marks matching, sew each red nose unit to an orange tail unit. Repeat with the green nose units and the teal tail units. Press the seams toward the yellow strip in each unit (Fig. 5). Trim the excess dark blue rectangle even with the triangle edges (Fig. 6).

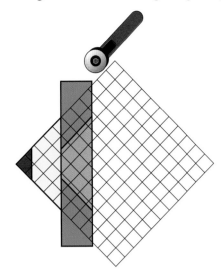

Fig. 6
Trim tail units even with
nose unit edges.

Step 9. Sew an aqua background triangle to each pieced fish unit. Note that the aqua triangles are cut oversize (see Fig. 7 on page 88). Press the seam toward the aqua triangle. You should have a total of 32 blocks, 16 of each color combination.

Miter That Border Corner

1. Mark the center at each edge of the quilt top and the raw edge of the inner border on each set of borders. Measure the quilt top through the center and subtract ½ inch.

2. Mark the length determined in Step 2 at the raw edge of the assembled border strip. Mark the center of the strip.

3. Carefully mark the ¼-inch seam intersection at each corner on the wrong side of the quilt top.

4. Pin a border to the quilt top with centers matching and the end marks matching the quilt-top seam intersections. Stitch, *beginning and ending the seam carefully at the seam intersections.* Press the seam toward the borders. Add the remaining borders in the same manner.

5. Fold the quilt top diagonally with right sides facing and the raw edges of the adjacent border strips aligned.

6. Position a rotary ruler along the fold and across the border strips and draw the stitching line (Fig. 12). Beginning at the seam intersection, stitch on the marked line. Trim the excess border ¼ inch from the stitching and press the seam open. Repeat to miter the remaining corners.

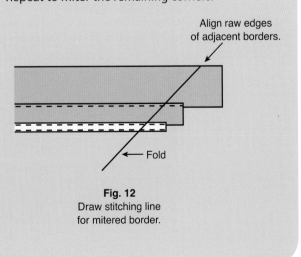

Align raw edges
of adjacent borders.

← Fold

Fig. 12
Draw stitching line
for mitered border.

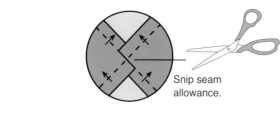

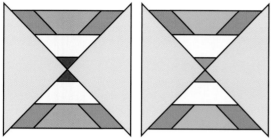

Fig. 7
Complete the Kissy Fish blocks.
Make 8 of each.

Step 10. Sew the units together in pairs to make "hourglass" blocks. Press the seams toward the aqua in each unit. To do so, carefully snip the center seam intersection so you can press the center seam in opposite directions in each block. This eliminates a bump in the center of the finished block (Fig. 7).

Step 11. Square blocks to 9 x 9 inches, making sure the kissing noses are centered in each one.

Step 12. Arrange the blocks in four rows of four blocks each, rotating the position of the fish as shown in Fig. 8. Sew the blocks together in rows and press the seams toward the aqua triangles in each row. Sew the rows together to create the center of the quilt top.

Step 13. Make a 45-degee-angle cut at one end of each of the four 3½ x 10-inch strips of dark blue print (Fig. 9).

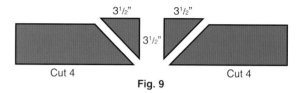

Fig. 9

Step 14. Sew triangles for the pieced middle border together as shown to make four identical strips. Add a dark blue piece from Step 13 to each end (Fig. 10).

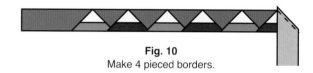

Fig. 10
Make 4 pieced borders.

Step 15. Fold each border strip (inner, middle, and outer) in half and mark the centers for matching. Sew the strips together with centers matching to make four border strips. Press all seams toward the outer border in each set of borders (Fig. 11).

Fig. 8
Kissy Fish Quilt Assembly

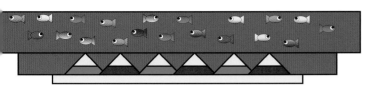

Fig. 11
Sew borders together,
matching centers.

Step 16. Sew the strips to the quilt top and miter the corners as directed in the sidebar on page 87.

Step 17. Layer the quilt top with batting and backing and baste the layers together. Quilt as desired.

Step 18. Optional: For sparkly eyes, add Swarovski crystals to each fish nose with a hot-fix wand.

Step 19. Join the binding strips with bias seams and press open. Fold the strip in half with wrong sides together and press. Bind the quilt, using a ⅜-inch-wide seam allowance. ❖

SHELL SEEKERS PORCH SET CONTINUED FROM PAGE 80

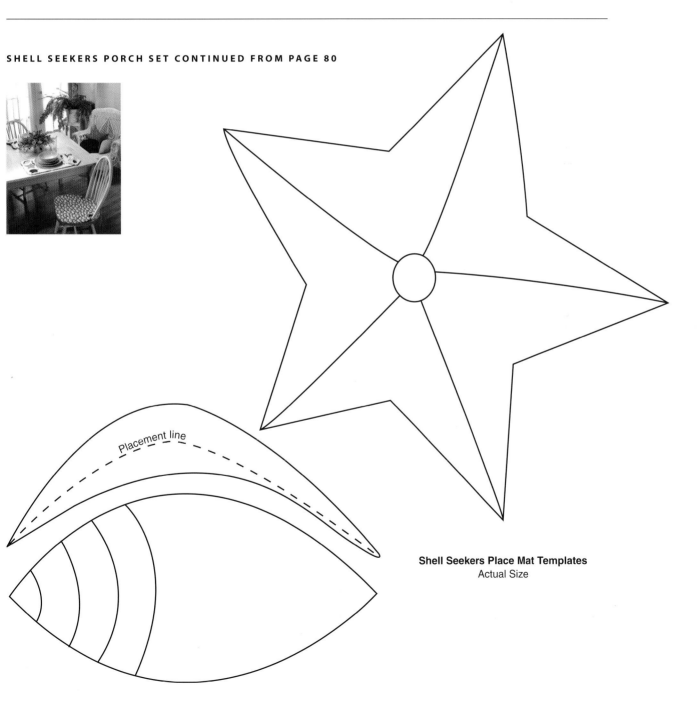

Placement line

Shell Seekers Place Mat Templates
Actual Size

Splish-Splash Swim Cover-Up

This cute cover-up is a great project to help children make for themselves. Purchase already-embroidered towels or use your embroidery machine to personalize the cover-up with some special details. The pink towel was already embellished with the band and butterfly trim.

DESIGN BY HOPE YODER

Project Specifications

Size: Fits children ages 5 to 8

Materials

- 1 towel 27 x 49 inches
- 1 coordinating hand towel
- Size 100 topstitching needle
- Purchased trims for embellishments
- All-purpose thread to match towel
- Rotary cutter, mat and ruler
- Basic sewing tools and equipment
- Embroidery sewing machine and your favorite designs, tear-away or water-soluble stabilizer, and iron-away stabilizer (optional)

Instructions

Step 1. Fold the towel in half and then in half again to find the center. Mark with a pin.

Step 2. Place straight pins 5½ inches to the right and left of center. Make an 11-inch-long slit along the center fold (Fig.1).

Step 3. Serge- or zigzag-finish the cut edges of the slit to prevent raveling during laundering. After finishing the edge, turn under and press ¼ inch around the slit opening and pin in place.

Step 4. Insert the topstitching needle in the machine and stitch ⅛ inch from the turned edge.

Fig. 1
Slash the folded edge between pins.

Step 5. If you plan to add an embroidered motif to the hood, embroider the hand towel now. Center the motif along one long edge of the towel and about 2 inches above the edge.

Step 6. Fold the hand towel in half crosswise with right sides together and finished short ends even. Trim to 10½ inches wide (Fig. 2).

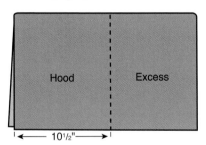

Fig. 2
Cut hood panel from folded hand towel.

Step 7. With the towel still folded, serge the raw edges together or stitch ¼ inch from the raw edges and finish the seam with zigzag stitch. Press the seam to one side and turn the hood right side out. Add trim to the opening edge of the hood if desired.

Step 8. Make two tucks at the neckline edge of the hood, spacing them as shown in Fig. 3. Machine baste ½ inch from the neckline edge of the hood, stitching through the tucks to secure them.

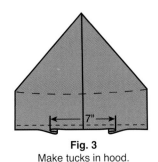

Fig. 3
Make tucks in hood.

Step 9. Fold the large towel in half lengthwise and place a pin at the center back.

Step 10. With the seam at the center back pin, tuck the neck edge of the hood under the finished edge of the neckline opening in the towel. Place the opening edge along the machine basting and pin in place.

Step 11. Adjust the machine for a 3.5mm stitch and topstitch the towel to the hood.

Step 12. Cut a 6-inch square from the leftover strip from the hand towel and use the finished edge for the upper edge of the pocket. Add an embroidered motif to the pocket square if desired.

Step 13. Add optional trim to the upper edge of the pocket now. Turn under and press ¼ inch at two side edges and the bottom edge of the pocket. Position on the front of the towel and pin. Edgestitch in place.

Step 14. With the towel folded in half with wrong sides together, measure 10½ inches from the fold and pin the layers together from this point to the lower edge. Stitch the pinned area ¼ inch from the edges of the towel (Fig. 4). ❖

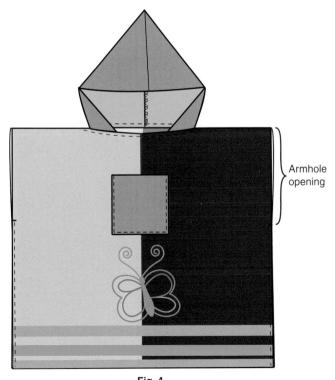

Fig. 4
Sew edges together below armhole marks.

Autumn Accents

The warm, rich tones of fall are reflected in this selection of projects. As the days begin to shorten and the leaves begin to float earthward, carve out some time at your sewing machine to create wardrobe items and home decor in this seasonal theme.

Felted Fancy Sweater Bag

Toss an old wool sweater into your washer and dryer to create beautiful sweater felt for this chic little handbag. It's astounding what hot water, soap and a little agitation can do to woolen fabric!

DESIGN BY LUCY B. GRAY

Project Specifications
Bag Size: Approximately 7 x 8 x 3 inches

Materials
- Discarded 100 percent wool sweater (from your closet or thrift store)
- ⅓ yard cotton fabric in coordinating or contrasting print for lining and ruffle
- 3-inch square color-coordinated leather or imitation-suede fabric
- 3-inch square polyester fleece
- Leather strap with metal snap-clasps from a thrift-store bag
- Decorative pin or brooch (optional)
- All-purpose thread to match fabrics
- 2 (½-inch-diameter) metal D-rings
- 1 magnetic snap set
- 4-inch square plastic from a clean milk jug
- 2 (¾-inch-diameter) buttons
- 2 (½-inch-diameter) metal buttons
- Pattern tracing cloth or paper
- Rotary cutter, mat and ruler
- Spray-on fabric protector
- Quick-drying fabric glue
- Craft scissors
- Craft knife
- Size 14 Universal sewing machine needle
- Basic sewing tools and equipment

Instructions

Step 1. Felt the sweater as directed in the sidebar on page 97. Cut the sweater apart along the seam lines and decide which side of the felted fabric you will use for the right side of the finished bag. The wrong side usually looks less knitted. You don't have to worry about the grain of the felt; it is fairly stable in all directions. The felted fabric will not ravel, so exposed raw-edge construction is appropriate.

Step 2. Referring to Fig. 1, make the bag pattern pieces on pattern tracing paper or cloth and cut out.

Step 3. Position the pattern pieces on the felted sweater pieces and trace around them, then cut out. Use rotary-cutting tools for clean, straight cuts. If necessary, cut the gusset in two pieces and remember to add a ⅜-inch-wide seam allowance to one short end of each piece. ***Note:*** *If your sweater has a pocket, salvage it for an inside pocket in the bag by cutting around it 1 inch beyond the pocket edges (Fig. 2).*

Fig. 2
Cut pocket from felted sweater
with 1" margin all around.

Step 4. Cut out the lining using the same pattern pieces. Spray each lining piece several times with fabric protector and allow to dry after each application.

Step 5. Adjust the sewing machine for a longer-than-average stitch and moderate pressure on the presser foot. Stitch two layers of felt scrap together to test the machine settings. Use a walking foot if available. If not, use lots of pins to secure the layer and keep them from shifting while stitching.

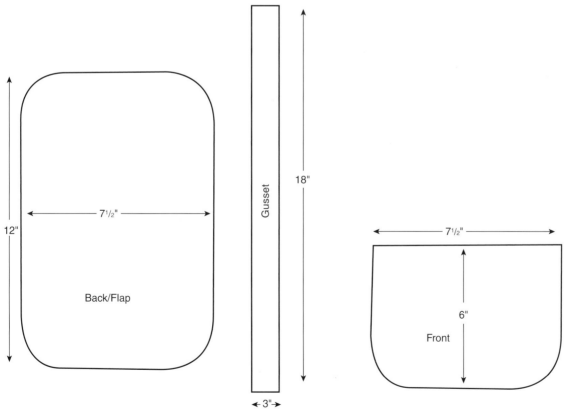

Fig. 1
Make bag pattern.

Step 6. If you salvaged a pocket for the lining, cut a hole in the lining piece the same size as the pocket, excluding the 1-inch margin all around. Machine baste ½ inch from the window edges and clip the corners to the stitching (Fig. 3). Turn under and press the opening edges along the basting. Center the pocket panel under the opening and stitch in place around the opening edges (Fig. 4).

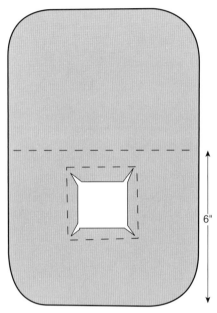

Fig. 3
Cut pocket window in
lower half of lining.

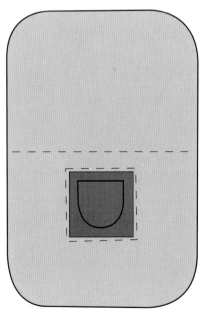

Fig. 4
Edgestitch lining
to pocket.

Step 7. If the felt gusset was cut in two pieces, sew the two short ends together using a ⅜-inch-wide seam allowance; press open. This seam may be stitched with wrong sides together so the seam allowances are on the right side of the gusset. It's your choice. Press the seam open.

Step 8. The lining pieces will probably be too large because of the difference in fabric weights. Place the back lining piece face up on the wrong side of the felt bag back and smooth it flat with the raw edges of the ovals even at the upper edge. Use a few pins to secure the layers, then carefully flip them over on your rotary-cutting mat and trim the lining even with the felt edges. Repeat with the gusset and the bag front pieces.

Step 9. With right sides together and centers matching at the lower edge, sew the lining gusset to the lining back using a ½-inch-wide seam allowance. With centers matching, sew the lining front to the lining gusset using a ½-inch-wide seam allowance (Fig. 5). Press the seams toward the gusset.

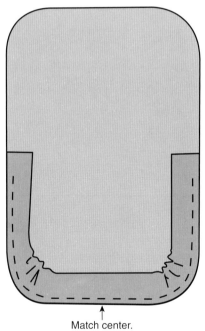

Match center.
Fig. 5
Sew lining gusset to
lining back/flap.

Step 10. With wrong sides together (so bag seam allowances are on the outside), pin the felt gusset to the felt front and back pieces. Sew together with ⅜-inch-wide seams.

Step 11. For the gathered ruffle, cut enough ¾-inch-wide true-bias strips of the lining fabric to make a continuous strip about 40 inches long. Overlap the bias ends and machine baste to make one long strip. Machine baste ¼ inch from one long raw edge (Fig. 6). Draw up the bobbin thread to gather the strip into a tight ruffle. Position the raw edge of the felt flap just below the basting stitches on the ruffle so that the ruffle extends a scant ½ inch beyond the flap edge. Pin in place. On the wrong side of the flap,

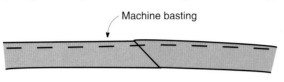

Machine basting

Fig. 6
Overlap bias ends and topstitch.

handsew the ruffle in place, embedding the stitches in the felt without allowing them to show on the right side (Fig. 7 on page 98).

Step 12. With wrong sides together, place the lining inside the bag, smoothing it so that the two layers fit together with as few wrinkles as possible. Turn under the raw edges of the lining around the bag opening edge so they lie a scant ¼ inch below the felt edges. Leaving a 2-inch section unstitched at the center front, slipstitch the lining in place; take care that the stitches don't show on the outside of the bag.

Step 13. Turn under the lining raw edge around the flap and slipstitch in place along the ruffle stitching. Leave a 2-inch section unstitched at the center of the flap.

Make It Felt: Sweater Felting 101

Any sweater that is 100 percent wool will felt, and some will felt more than others. I've had the best luck felting crew-neck sweaters knit with Shetland wool. This sweater style also yields the most felted yardage since the front and back are simply styled. Raid your closet for "volunteers" or hit your local thrift shop to find just the right sweater for this project.

Felting wool goes counter to everything you've learned about laundering it. You can expect a 100 percent wool sweater to shrink up to half its size and become very thick and soft using the following method.

1. Set the washing machine for the hottest water temperature and add ¼ cup inexpensive shampoo to the water.

2. Use a 30-minute wash cycle and machine dry the sweater at the hottest temperature until it is barely damp. Check to make sure it is

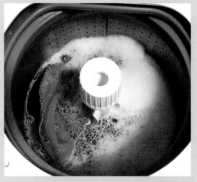

sufficiently felted. If not, wash and dry again. When the sweater has shrunk sufficiently and is about ¼ inch thick, remove it from the dryer and pat it flat on a smooth surface. Allow to air-dry. The shampoo removes the hard finish that dry cleaning leaves behind on garments and restores a soft, satiny luster to the wool fibers.

BEFORE

AFTER

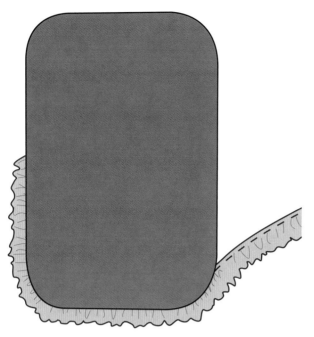

Fig. 7
Tack raw edge of ruffle under flap
edge and hand-sew in place.

between the lining and the felt, place the perforated metal disk, then the plastic over the prongs and bend them to the outside. Glue a 1½ x 2½-inch piece of fleece on top of the prongs and plastic inside for padding. Determine the position for the female snap by closing the flap and observing where the male snap lies on the felt front of the bag. Mark it with a pin, and install the female snap exactly the same way. Slipstitch both openings closed.

Step 15. Cut two 1 x 2½-inch ovals from leather or imitation suede. Thread each through a metal D-ring and fold in half. Use glue stick to temporarily adhere a ¾-inch-diameter button to each piece.

Step 16. Place the leather and ring on the inside of the bag at the upper edge of the gusset with the ring just above the lining edge. Place a small metal button on the outside of the bag and a larger button inside on the leather and sew all the way through both buttons several times.

Step 14. Cut three 1 x 2-inch pieces of milk-jug plastic for reinforcements for the magnetic snaps. Using one of the perforated metal disks that came with the snaps and a craft knife, cut the openings for the snap prongs in two of the plastic pieces. Slip the remaining plastic piece between the lining and felt flap layers to protect the felt when cutting. Mark the openings for the snap prongs on the flap lining about ½ inch below the edge. Cut two slits in the lining, and push the male snap prongs through. Reaching through the opening

Step 17. Add a long strap with metal snap-clasps, recycled from a used bag, or make one from fabric or leather.

Step 18: Add a dramatic focal point to your sweater bag with a decorative pin or brooch, chosen to complement both the color and style of the bag. ❖

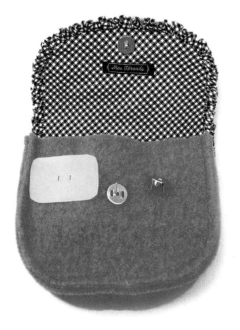

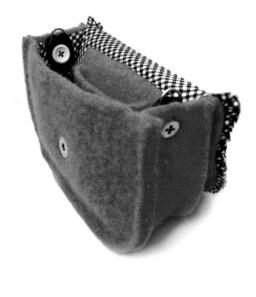

Loop Tricks
& Pick-Up Stix

Wool-and-rayon felt is the perfect medium for these graphic pillows that are easy to sew and oh-so-soft to the touch.

DESIGNS BY KAREN DILLON

Project Specifications

Loop Tricks Pillow Size: 14 inches square
Pick-Up Stix Pillow Size: 14 inches square

Materials
Loop Tricks Pillow

- 16 x 36-inch piece black wool or wool-blend felt for pillow cover front and back
- 16 x 36-inch piece red felt for loops

Pick-Up Stix Pillow

- 16 x 36-inch piece red felt for the pillow cover front and back
- 7 x 30-inch strip pink felt for the stix

Both Pillows

- All-purpose thread to match felt
- 14-inch square pillow form for each pillow
- Rotary cutter, mat and ruler
- Tailor's chalk or white dressmaker's pencil
- Pinking shears or rotary cutter with wavy blade
- Basic sewing tools and equipment

Instructions
Loop Tricks

Step 1. From the black felt, cut two 14¾-inch squares. From the red felt, cut eleven 1¼ x 36-inch strips.

Step 2. Using tailor's chalk or a white dressmaker's pencil, draw a line ½ inch from each raw edge of one black square.

Step 3. Using the chalk pencil, draw parallel lines ⅞ inch apart in the interior of the square (Fig. 1).

Step 4. Beginning at the left edge of the black square, position a red strip with the short end even with the upper raw edge of the square and the left-hand edge even with the seam line. Pin in place. Add the remaining strips in the same manner with the right-hand edge of the right strip even with the seam

line on the right edge of the square. Stitch ½ inch from the raw edges to anchor the strips to the square.

Step 5. Using the chalk or chalk pencil, draw lines across the strips, spacing them 2 inches apart (Fig. 2).

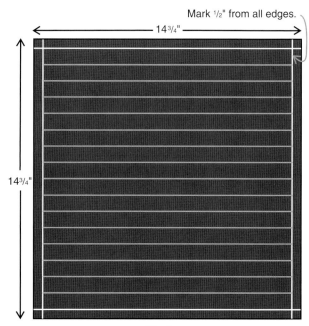

Mark ½" from all edges.
14¾"
14¾"

Fig. 1
Draw lines ⅞" apart across felt square.

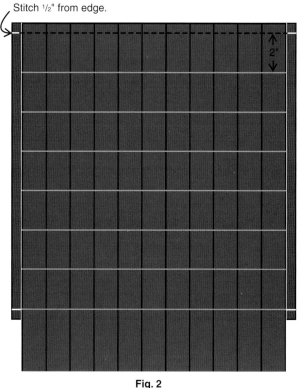

Stitch ½" from edge.
2"

Fig. 2
Draw lines 2" apart across strips.

Step 6. To make the first row of loops, bring the first line on each strip in line with the first line on the background square. Pin in place. Using your fingers to hold the loops out of the way, stitch on the line across the loops (Fig. 3).

Match lines on strips to lines on background square and stitch.

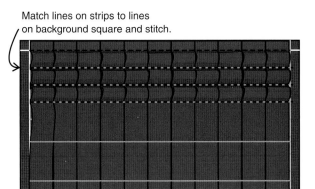

Fig. 3
Making Loops

Step 7. Continue making and stitching each row of loops in the same manner. Trim the ends of the strips even with the raw edges of the pillow top.

Step 8. With the wrong side of the looped square against the wrong side of the remaining black square and raw edges even, stitch ½ inch from three of the four edges. Trim the three seams to ¼ inch using the pinking shears or wavy rotary-cutter blade.

Step 9. Insert the pillow form through the open edge and pin the opening edges together. Stitch ½ inch from the raw edges and pink the edge.

Pick-Up Stix Pillow

Step 1. From the red felt, cut two pieces each 15 inches square. From the pink felt, cut ½-inch-wide strips. Cut into 54 strips in assorted lengths of 4–6 inches.

Step 2. Using tailor's chalk or the white dressmaker's pencil, draw a line ½ inch from the raw edges of one red square.

Step 3. Arrange the pink strips in three rows of 18 strips each on the pillow top (see photo) and secure each one with a straight pin. Some should tilt and you may trim a few strips a bit narrower for added visual interest.

Step 4. When pleased with the arrangement, stitch close to all four edges of each strip (Fig. 4).

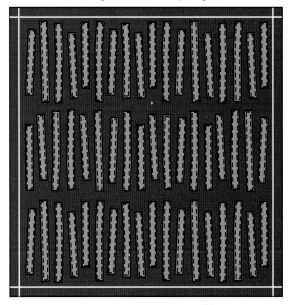

Fig. 4
Stitch close to edges.

Step 5. With the wrong side of the finished square against the wrong side of the remaining red square and raw edges even, stitch ½ inch from three of the four edges of the squares. Trim the three seams to ¼ inch using the pinking shears or wavy rotary-cutter blade.

Step 6. Insert the pillow form through the open edge, pin and then stitch the open edges together. Pink the edge. ❖

Make It Yours

Change the colors to create your own version of these fun pillows. Cut the "stix" from more than one color felt. Or, use ribbons instead of felt strips to create a festive holiday version of the loopy pillow.

Quick-Change Pillow Toppers

You can change the look of this pillow with a flick of your wrist when you make two or more shaped, button-on toppers. Choose two different fabrics for two different looks. Or cut the lining for each topper from yet another fabric to make them reversible and create even more options for your seasonal decorating.

DESIGN BY CAROL ZENTGRAF

Project Specifications

Pillow Size: 16 inches square

Materials

Project Note: *Materials given are for one pillow and two toppers. Yardages are for 54-inch-wide decorator fabrics.*

- ½ yard for the pillow cover
- ½ yard for tasseled topper or fringe-trimmed topper
- 17-inch square of light- to medium-weight fusible interfacing for topper
- 3 tassels with hanging loops for tasseled topper
- ⅔ yard eyelash fringe for fringe-trimmed topper
- One 16-inch-square pillow form
- 6 (⅞-inch-diameter) button forms for covered buttons
- Permanent fabric adhesive
- Pattern tracing cloth or tissue
- Dressmaker's pencil
- All-purpose sewing thread to match fabrics
- Point turner
- Basic sewing tools and equipment

Make It Yours

If you like this quick-change idea, you can create even more decorating versatility by trying some of these designing strategies:

- Make extra pillow covers in coordinating fabrics for mix-and-match options.
- Line the pillow with a different fabric to make it reversible.
- Cut the lining for each topper from a contrasting fabric.
- Shape the back edge of the topper to match the shape of the front edge.

Instructions

Project Note: *All seam allowances are ½ inch wide.*

Step 1. Cut two 17-inch squares from the fabric for the pillow cover. Cut two 17-inch squares from each topper fabric.

Step 2. Enlarge the topper patterns (Figs. 1 and 2) on pattern tracing cloth or tissue, and cut out.

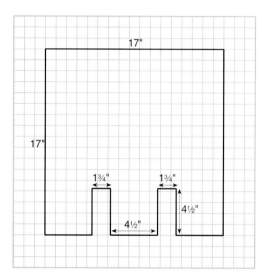

Fig. 1
1 square = 1"

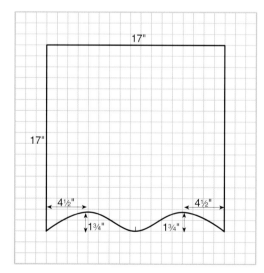

Fig. 2
1 square = 1"

Step 3. With right sides together, stitch the two squares for the pillow cover together ½ inch from three edges. Clip the corners and turn right side out. Press the edges. Make a double ½-inch-wide hem at the remaining raw edge.

Step 4. Apply fusible interfacing to the wrong side of one square for each topper following the manufacturer's directions.

Step 5. Layer the topper pieces with right sides together and raw edges even. Pin the topper pattern piece in place and cut both layers along the shaped edges.

Step 6. *For the tasseled topper:* Center tassels in each shaped section with the tassel heads ¾ inch from the shaped edge on the right side of one of the two pieces. Baste the tassel loops in place (Fig. 3).

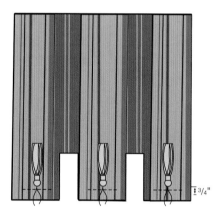

Fig. 3
Sew tassels in place.

Step 7. *For both toppers:* Beginning close to the center of the edge opposite the shaped edge, sew the topper panels together. Leave a 4-inch-long opening for turning. Trim the seams to ⅜ inch and trim across the outer corners to eliminate bulk. Clip the inward curves and corners to but not past the stitching (Fig. 4). Turn right side out and use a point turner (not the point of your scissors) to create smoothly turned corners; press. Turn under and press the opening edge. Topstitch ¼ inch from the edge.

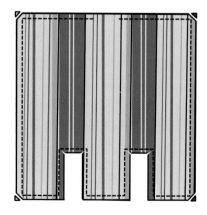

Fig. 4
Stitch; clip corners.

Step 8. *To finish the tasseled topper:* Make a 1-inch-long buttonhole in the center of each flap section. Buttonholes should end ¾ inch from the flap lower edge. Fold the topper in half crosswise with side edges aligned and mark the buttonhole positions on the back of the topper. Make 1-inch-long buttonholes at the marks.

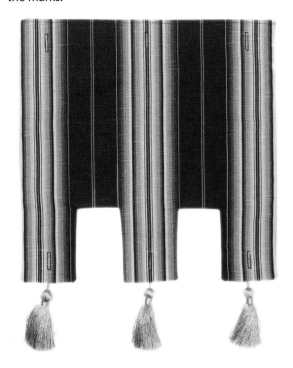

Step 9. *To finish the fringed topper:* Make three 1-inch-long vertical buttonholes above the shaped, fringed edge. Position one at the center of the topper and the outer ones 1¾ inches from the outer finished edges. Buttonholes should end ¾ inch from the flap lower edge. Mark and make buttonholes at the opposite edge of the topper. Glue or sew eyelash fringe to the front curved edge.

Step 10. Fold the tasseled topper over the open end of the pillow cover, positioning the front edge as desired. Using the dressmaker's pencil, mark the button placements under the buttonholes on the pillow-cover front only.

Step 11. Follow the package directions to make six covered buttons, using scraps of the pillow fabric. Sew three buttons in place on the pillow- cover front.

Step 12. For a softer pillow, open one side seam of the pillow form and remove about half of the stuffing. Machine stitch the opening closed. Insert the pillow in the pillow cover and button the tasseled topper in place. Wrap the other edge over the pillow-cover opening and mark the button positions beneath the buttonholes. Remove the pillow form and sew the buttons in place on the back of the pillow cover. ❖

Something to Crow About
Penny Rug

This proud rooster is ready to crow and you will be too when you see how easy it is to cut and stitch a penny rug for your fall table centerpiece.

DESIGN BY PAMELA CECIL

Project Specifications
Penny Rug Size: 13½ x 17½ inches

Materials
- ⅝ yard black wool felt
- ¼ yard each of wool felt in the following colors: crimson, off-white, yellow, bronze, pumpkin, copper, denim blue, moss green, gold
- Embroidery floss in the following colors: gold, yellow, light yellow, medium moss green, orange, burgundy, black, medium blue
- Paper-backed lightweight fusible web
- Pattern tracing cloth or tissue
- White chalk pencil for marking on black
- Press cloth
- Chenille/candlewicking needle
- Scraps of poster board or template plastic
- Sharp scissors
- Pencil
- Straight pins

Instructions
Step 1. Trace all templates on page 109 and 110 onto poster board or template plastic and cut out.

Step 2. Using the dimensions given in Fig. 1, draw a complete oval onto pattern tracing cloth or tissue. Fold the black felt in half and pin the pattern in place. Cut out two ovals and set aside.

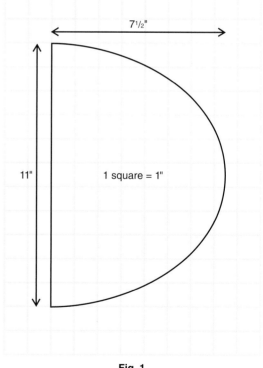

Fig. 1
Oval Pattern

7½"

11"

1 square = 1"

Step 3. Use a sharp white chalk pencil to trace around the large half-circle tab 16 times on the doubled black felt. Cut out the sets of tabs and place a straight pin through each set as it is cut to keep the mates together.

Step 4. Referring to the templates on page 110 and the small half-circle tab template on page 109, trace the required number of each piece onto the paper side of the fusible web. Group pieces for each color and leave ¼ inch of space between the pieces. Cut out the pieces in groups and apply the fusible web to the appropriate-color felt. Cut out each felt piece and remove the paper backing.

Step 5. Referring to the photo and the templates on page 110, position the felt pieces in numerical order on one black oval. Fuse in place following the manufacturer's directions.

Step 6. For the tabs, fuse the eight small yellow and eight small copper half-circle tabs to the upper black tab in each set. Align the straight edges before fusing. Re-pin the tab sets together as you compete each one.

Step 7. Using 3 strands of embroidery floss and referring to Fig. 2, blanket stitch around each piece of felt using the following colors:
• Black for rooster body
• Gold for sunflower stems, second tail feather and middle wing feather
• Yellow for fourth tail feather and first wing feather

• Orange for sunflower buds, sunflower bloom and rooster beak and feet
• Burgundy for sunflower center and the six small circles
• Light yellow for the rooster comb and wattle
• Medium moss green for the first tail feather and the third wing feather
• Medium blue for the first wing feather and the third and fifth tail feather.

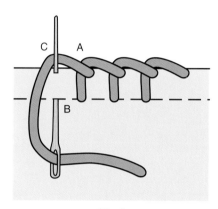

Fig. 2
Blanket Stitch

Step 8. Using 3 strands of black floss, stitch a French knot through all layers in the center of the rooster's eye.

Step 9. Use 3 strands of orange floss to blanket stitch around the curved edge of the yellow half-circle tabs on the black tabs, stitching through the top black layer only in each tab pair. Use the burgundy floss to stitch the copper half-circle tabs in the same manner.

Step 10. Use 3 strands of orange floss and make long cross-stitches to embroider the two large stars (Fig. 4) above the rooster. Using 3 strands of gold floss, make the smaller star between the two larger ones.

Fig. 4
Embroider 1 small and 2 large stars

Step 11. Holding the tabs in matched pairs, use 3 strands of moss green floss to blanket stitch around the outer curved edges of each pair of black tabs.

Step 12. On the remaining black oval, arrange the tabs around the outer edge of the oval with the tab ends extending ¼ inch over the oval edge. The side edges of the tabs may overlap each other slightly so that all

Perfect Points

To make neat stitches when turning corners or stitching around sharp points (feathers and comb tips), take a tiny extra stitch to tack down the blanket stitch at the tip. Bring the needle up from the back at the tip, catch the floss and insert the needle at the tip. Bring the needle back up at the tip and catch a few of the felt fibers to ensure that the tacking is secure (Fig. 3). Continue with the blanket stitching.

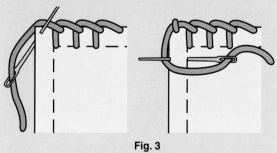

Fig. 3
Insert needle at tip
to anchor blanket stitch at corner.

tabs fit neatly around the oval. Pin in place and then baste, using 1 strand of black embroidery floss.

Step 13. Position the appliquéed oval on top and pin in place. Use 3 strands of the moss green floss to blanket stitch around the edges of the upper oval, catching the tabs in the stitching. Repeat on the reverse side, catching the back of the tabs in the stitching. ❖

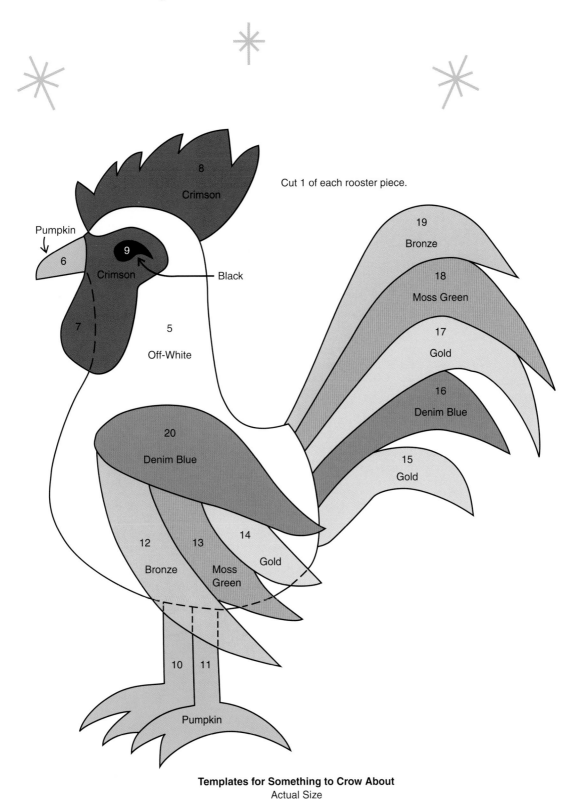

Cut 1 of each rooster piece.

Templates for Something to Crow About
Actual Size

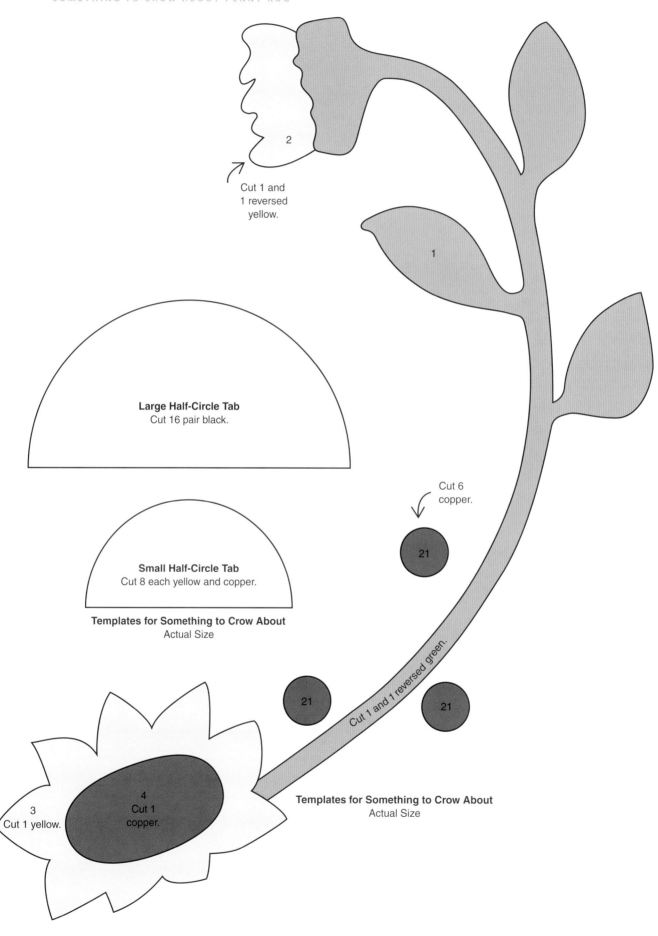

Cut 1 and
1 reversed
yellow.

2

Large Half-Circle Tab
Cut 16 pair black.

Small Half-Circle Tab
Cut 8 each yellow and copper.

Templates for Something to Crow About
Actual Size

Cut 6
copper.

21

21

21

Cut 1 and 1 reversed green.

3
Cut 1 yellow.

4
Cut 1
copper.

Templates for Something to Crow About
Actual Size

Juice-Can Jazz Footstool

Recycled juice cans create the perfect shape for a jazzy little fabric-covered footstool for your porch or patio.

DESIGN BY CAROL ZENTGRAF

Project Specifications

Footstool Size: 8 x 14 inches

Materials

Project Note: *Yardage is for decorator fabrics.*

- 18 x 36-inch piece floral print for top and bottom
- 9 x 17-inch piece each of three coordinating checks or plaids for the side panel
- 10 x 48-inch piece low-loft polyester batting for sides
- 18-inch square piece high-loft polyester batting for top
- 3 yards tasseled fringe with decorative header
- 7 large juice cans (approximately 7 inches tall and 4½ inches in diameter)
- Gorilla Glue
- Permanent fabric adhesive
- 14-inch square of template plastic or cardboard
- Punch-style can opener
- Air-soluble marking pen
- Spray adhesive (fabric-compatible)

Instructions

Step 1. Use the punch-style can opener to make two holes opposite each other on one end of each can. *Do not remove the end of the can.* Empty the cans, rinse thoroughly and allow to dry.

Step 2. Arrange the cans as shown in Fig. 1 and glue together with Gorilla Glue following the package directions. Allow to dry several hours or overnight.

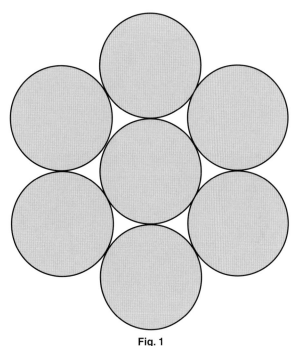

Fig. 1
Glue cans together.

Step 3. For a cutting template, trace around the scalloped outline of the combined cans on template plastic or cardboard; cut out.

Step 4. Fold the floral fabric in half with right sides together to make an 18-inch square. Place the template on the folded fabric and trace around the outer edges with the marking pen. Measure and mark a cutting line *2 inches beyond the traced outline*. Pin the fabric layers together and cut the shape from both layers following the outer line.

Step 5. Cut two 8½ x 9-inch rectangles from each plaid and checked fabric.

Step 6. Use the cardboard template as a pattern to cut one high-loft batting shape for the top.

Step 7. Working in a well-ventilated area, apply a coat of spray adhesive to the sides and tops of the cans. Position the high-loft batting on top and the strip of low-loft batting around the side of the footstool. Trim as needed.

Step 8. Center one floral fabric piece on the top of the batting-covered stool. Wrap the fabric over the edges and onto the footstool side, clipping as needed. Glue in place with fabric adhesive.

Step 9. Arrange the 8½ x 9-inch fabric rectangles in the desired order. With right sides together, sew the 9-inch-long edges of the rectangles together to make one long strip. Sew the remaining two edges together to create a circle of fabric.

Step 10. Slip the fabric circle over the cans with the upper fabric edge even with the tops of the cans and the seams positioned at the inner curves where the cans connect with each other. Use fabric adhesive to glue the fabric to the batting along the edges

Step 11. Spray both sides of the cardboard template with adhesive. Center it on the wrong side of the remaining floral fabric piece. Wrap the fabric edge around the cardboard, clipping as needed and finger-press in place. With the fabric side out, glue the cardboard to the bottom of the cans using fabric adhesive.

Step 12. Use fabric adhesive to glue two rows of tasseled fringe around the tops of the cans, covering the fabric raw edge. ❖

Can Do!

Use this technique to make footstools in other sizes or shapes. Use fabrics in color combinations that reflect your decorating palette.

• Use paint cans to make a larger stool. Buy new ones at your hardware or home-supply store. Remove the handles and tap the lid into place.

• Glue three cans together to make a triangular shape.

• Glue four cans together to make a square or diamond shape (Fig. 2).

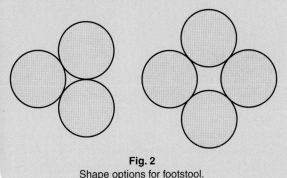

Fig. 2
Shape options for footstool.

Leaf-Peeper's Jacket

Hand-over-dyed wool is a wonderful backdrop for falling leaves on this comfy little cardigan jacket. It's perfect for an excursion to enjoy the fall scenery— or for shopping or lunching with friends on a crisp autumn day.

DESIGN BY MARY AYRES

Project Specifications
Jacket Size: Your size

Materials
- Cardigan jacket pattern of your choice (New Look pattern #6290 used for model)
- Pattern tracing cloth or tissue
- 1 (16 x 26-inch) piece wool in each of the following colors: gray, tan and red
- 2 (16 x 26-inch) pieces wool in each of the following colors: black, brown, green,
- 2 skeins of black embroidery floss
- All-purpose thread to match fabrics for jacket body
- Glue stick
- Pencil
- Basic sewing tools and equipment

Instructions
Project Notes: *Measurements for the piecing sections on the jacket front and sleeves are for a size 10. Adjust the size of the pieced sections for larger sizes if desired. You may also need to adjust the section sizes for a more pleasing proportion on other jacket styles and lengths.*

For larger sizes, consider cutting and appliquéing a cascade of additional leaves down the jacket front.

To finish raw edges, stitch and pink the edges or serge-finish them.

Step 1. Referring to Fig. 1 and the jacket photo, draw lines on the jacket front and sleeve pattern pieces to

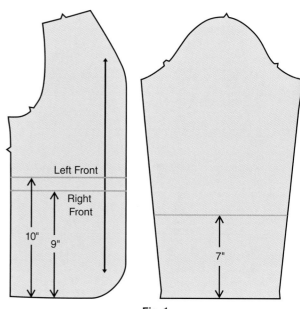

Fig. 1
Draw lines on pattern pieces.

divide them into piecing sections. On the jacket front there are two lines, one for the right front and one for the left front. Trace the sections onto pattern tracing cloth or tissue and add ⅝-inch-wide seam allowances as shown in Fig 2.

Step 2. Cut the front and sleeve pieces from the colors as shown in the photo. Cut the back from the black wool.

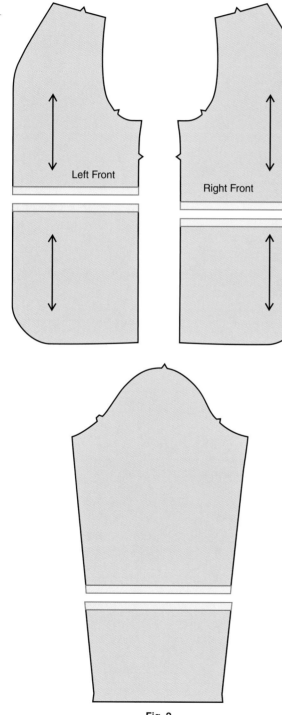

Left Front

Right Front

Fig. 2
Add seam allowances.

Step 3. Sew the upper front pieces to the lower front pieces, press the seams open and trim to ¼ inch with pinking shears.

Step 4. Sew the upper sleeves to the lower sleeves and press the seams open. Trim with pinking shears.

Step 5. Assemble the jacket following the pattern guide sheet.

Step 6. Use 6 strands of black embroidery floss to whipstitch over the faced and hemmed edges of the jacket. (Hide knots between the jacket and facing or hem layers.) For evenly spaced stitches, machine baste with a long stitch ½ inch from the edges and use the stitches as a spacing guide for the width between the whipstitches. Remove the basting.

Step 7. Trace the leaves on page 117 onto template plastic and cut out.

Make It Yours

Use white or off-white wool snowflakes (Fig. 3) on shades of blue to make a wintry version of this cozy little jacket. Reduce and enlarge the snowflake to make a variety of snowflake sizes. Or make your own snowflake patterns using the folded-paper cutting technique you learned as a child. Embroider around the snowflake and jacket edges using charcoal-colored embroidery floss. For a spring jacket, use the same technique with pastel shades of wool.

Fig. 3
Enlarge and reduce as desired for varying sizes.

Step 8. Trace around the leaf templates on the appropriate-color fabric as directed on the templates; cut out.

Step 9. Refer to the jacket photo and arrange the leaves on the upper right front and

lower left front. Use glue stick or straight pins to hold leaves in place.

Step 10. Blanket stitch over the raw edges of the leaves using 3 strands of black embroidery floss. Angle the blanket stitches slightly to mimic the angle of the whipstitching over the jacket edges. Note that the stitches go over both edges of the stems. ❖

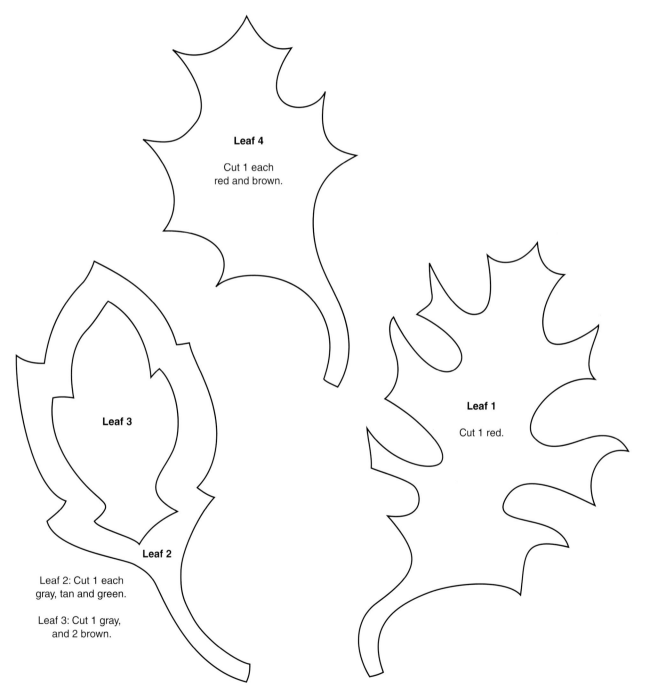

Leaf 4

Cut 1 each red and brown.

Leaf 3

Leaf 1

Cut 1 red.

Leaf 2

Leaf 2: Cut 1 each gray, tan and green.

Leaf 3: Cut 1 gray, and 2 brown.

Templates for Leaf Peepers
Actual Size

Falling Leaves Lap Quilt

Capture falling leaves in a cozy quilt to cuddle under on crisp autumn days. Quilting the panels before joining them with binding strips on the right side is an easier way to manage the weight of the quilt at the machine.

DESIGN BY PAM LINDQUIST

Project Specifications

Quilt Size: 63 x 76 inches

Materials

Project Note: *Yardages are for 44/45-inch-wide fabrics.*

- 3 yards medium brown print for strip panels
- 1¾ yards green stripe for strip panel borders, block borders and quilt binding
- 1½ yards total assorted autumn-colored prints for leaves
- 1½ yards total assorted off-white prints for leaf block backgrounds
- 5⅛ yards green or brown print for quilt backing
- 21 (3½-inch) squares of tissue paper for paper-piecing the stems
- 80 x 84-inch piece of batting or 16½ yards of 20-inch-wide batting
- All-purpose thread to match fabrics
- Walking foot (optional:)
- Basic sewing tools and equipment

Instructions

Project Notes: *Preshrink and press all fabrics before cutting. Use ¼-inch-wide seams to piece the leaf blocks and panels. All other seams are ½-inch wide unless otherwise noted.*

Step 1. From the medium brown print, cut four 10 x 76-inch strips. From the remaining fabric, cut two 10 x 42-inch strips. From these, cut a total of six 9½ x 10-inch rectangles.

Step 2. From the green stripe, cut the following strips across the fabric width: 12 strips each 2 x 42 inches for the vertical strip-panel binding and eight strips each 3 x 42 inches for the quilt binding. Cut six strips each 1 x 42 inches. From these strips, cut (24) 1 x 9½-inch strips for the sashing strips between the leaf blocks.

Step 3. From the backing fabric, cut seven 10 x 84-inch strips.

Step 4. From the assorted autumn-colored prints, cut: (21) ¾ x 4¼-inch rectangles for leaf stems, (42) 4-inch squares for half-square-triangle units and (63) 3½-inch squares for the leaf blocks.

Step 5. From the assorted off-white prints, cut: (42) 4-inch squares for half-square-triangle units, (21) 3½-inch squares for the block corners, (42) 2¼ x 4¼-inch rectangles for leaf stem squares and (21) 2 x 9-inch rectangles for leaf-block side strips.

Step 6. From the batting, cut seven strips each 10 x 84 inches.

Step 7. Draw a ¼-inch-wide stem diagonally on each tissue-paper square. Center a ¾ x 4¼-inch stem strip right side up over the drawn line on the tissue-paper pattern (Fig. 1).

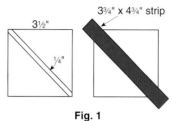

Fig. 1
Draw stem on tissue; center strip over lines.

Step 8. Align a 2¼ x 4¼-inch off-white fabric rectangle with raw edges even and right sides together along an edge of the leaf stem. Pin in place. Stitch ¼ inch from the raw edges through the fabrics and the tissue paper. Flip the fabric onto the tissue paper and press (Fig. 2).

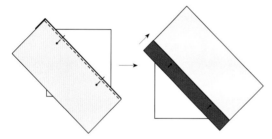

Fig. 2
Add background rectangle.

Step 9. Align a second 2¼ x 4¼-inch off-white fabric rectangle, right sides together, along the remaining raw edge of the stem. Sew in place, flip and press (Fig. 3). Make a total of 21 stem squares in this manner.

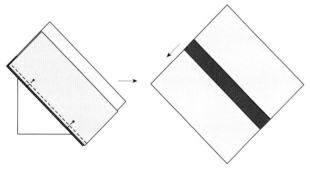

Fig. 3
Make 21 stem squares.

Step 10. Flip the piece over and use the tissue-paper edges as a guide to trim the block to 3½ inches square (Fig. 4). Carefully tear away the tissue paper.

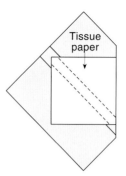

Fig. 4
Trim excess fabric along
tissue-paper edges.

Step 11. Pair a 4-inch autumn print square with an off-white 4-inch square and place right sides together. Use a pencil and ruler to draw a diagonal line from corner to corner on the wrong side of the lighter square. Stitch ¼ inch from the drawn line on each side and cut apart on the line to yield two units. Flip the darker triangle toward the seam allowance and press. Trim each unit to 3½ inch square (Fig. 5).

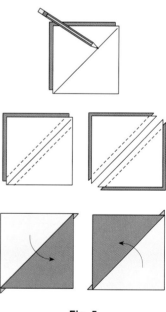

Fig. 5
Make half-square triangles.

Step 12. Arrange four 3½-inch half-square-triangle units with three autumn print 3½-inch squares, one 3½-inch off-white square and one 3½-inch leaf-stem square as shown in Fig. 6. Sew together in horizontal rows and press as directed by the arrows. Sew the rows together to complete the block. Repeat Steps 11 and 12 to make a total of 21 Autumn Leaf blocks.

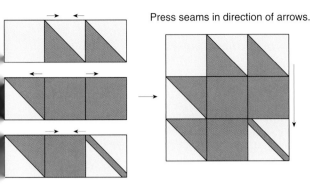

Press seams in direction of arrows.

Fig. 6
Make 21 Autumn Leaf blocks.

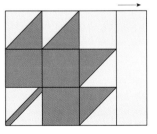

Step 15. To prepare each panel for quilting, place a backing panel face down and add a batting strip. Smooth the leaf panel in place on top and pin or hand baste the layers together. Quilt as desired. Trim the quilt batting and backing even with the edges of the pieced panel.

Step 13. Sew a 2 x 9-inch off-white rectangle to the right edge of nine Autumn Leaf blocks and to the left edge of the remaining 12 leaf blocks. Press as directed (Fig. 7).

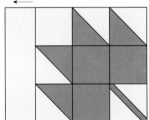

Fig. 7
Add strips and press.

Step 14. Arrange the leaf blocks in three rows with stem positions alternating as shown and 1 x 9½-inch striped sashing strips positioned between the blocks and at the top and bottom of each row. Add a 9½ x 10½-inch brown rectangle to the top and bottom of each row (Fig. 8). Sew the pieces together in rows, using ¼-inch-wide seams. Press the seams toward the sashing strips.

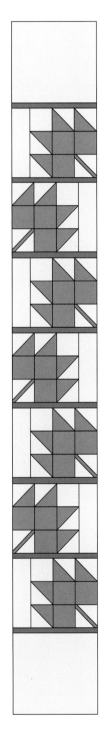

Fig. 8
Make 3 strips.

Step 16. Layer and quilt the brown print panels in the same manner. Trim the quilt batting and backing even with the edges of the brown print panels. Arrange the plain and pieced panels in alternating fashion, beginning and ending with a brown panel.

Step 17. Sew the 2-inch-wide binding strips together in pairs to make six long strips. Press the seams open and trim each strip to match the length (about 76 inches) of the quilted panels. Fold each strip in half with wrong sides together and press.

Step 18. With backing sides together, pin a leaf panel to a brown print panel back to back with a brown print panel. With raw edges even, position and pin a folded strip on the right side of the autumn leaf strip panel. Stitch ½ inch from the raw edges. Trim the batting and the seam allowances to ¼ inch (Fig. 9).

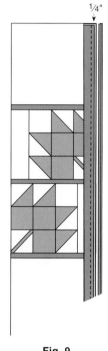

1/4"

Fig. 9
Stitch folded strip to layered panels. Trim to ¼".

Step 19. Press the seam allowance and binding strip toward the brown print panel. Slipstitch the folded edge of the binding to the brown print panel (Fig. 10). Repeat to join all remaining panels in the same manner.

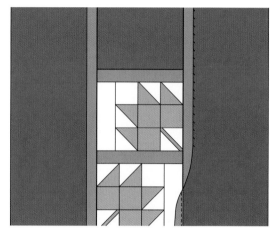

Fig. 10
Slipstitch binding to quilt.

Step 20. Sew the 3-inch-wide binding strips together using bias seams to make one strip approximately 290 inches long. Press the seams open. Fold the strip in half lengthwise with wrong sides together and press.

Step 21. Using a ½-inch-wide seam allowance and mitering the corners as you reach them, sew the binding to the quilt. Turn the folded edge of the binding over the raw edge of the quilt to the back and slipstitch in place, mitering the corners when you reach them. ❖

A Fall Welcome

Invite your guests to the pumpkin patch with this cheery door banner. Fuse the pumpkins and add machine stitched accents for quick and easy sewing.

BY JULIE WEAVER

Project Specifications

Banner Size: 25 x 54 inches

Materials

- ½ yard 44/45-inch-wide tan tone-on-tone print for appliqué background
- ⅝ yard 54-inch-wide small-check decorator fabric for pieced panel
- ½ yard 54-inch-wide decorator plaid for pieced panel
- 1⅔ yards 44/45-inch-wide fall print for lining
- 12-inch squares of three different orange tone-on-tone prints for pumpkins
- Scraps of two or three different green prints for leaves
- 6-inch square brown tone-on-tone print for stems
- 1 yard paper-backed fusible web
- Pencil
- Air-soluble marking pen or tailor's chalk
- Green and brown embroidery floss
- All-purpose thread to match fabrics
- Rotary cutter, mat and ruler
- Basic sewing tools and equipment

Instructions

Step 1. From the tan print, cut a 17½ x 26½-inch rectangle for the appliqué background.

Step 2. From the check fabric, cut three strips each 6½ x 39½ inches. From the plaid fabric, cut two strips each 6½ x 39½ inches. Cut one strip 6 x 24 inches for the hanging sleeve.

Step 3. Enlarge the pumpkin templates on pages 126 and 127 as directed and trace onto the paper side of the fusible web, leaving ½ inch of space between

them. Cut out each shape with a ¼-inch-wide margin beyond the drawn lines.

Step 4. Following the manufacturer's directions, fuse each piece to the wrong side of the appropriate fabric and cut out on the drawn lines. Remove the paper.

Step 5. Using the marking pen or chalk, draw the veins on the pumpkins and leaves.

Step 6. Referring to Fig. 1, position the appliqués in numerical order on the right side of the tan rectangle. Place the bottom edges of the two lower pumpkins 2¾ inches above the lower raw edge of the panel. Fuse in place following manufacturer's directions.

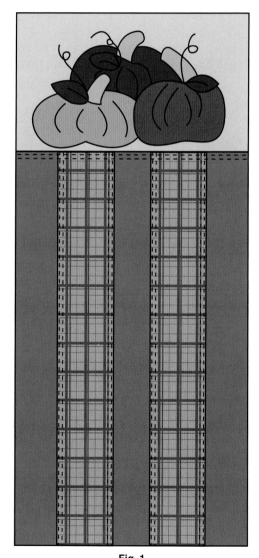

Fig. 1
Banner Assembly

Make It Easy

If available for your machine, use a walking foot when topstitching the pressed edge of flat-felled seams like those in this banner. It feeds the fabric layers evenly through the machine, eliminating tucks in the edge that can occur when using a regular presser foot. The open-toe embroidery foot and the edgestitching presser foot are other options that can make it easier to edgestitch the seams in place. For a more noticeable flat-felled seam, use a contrasting thread for stitching and topstitching the seam.

Step 7. Blanket stitch around each appliqué by hand or machine (see Fig. 2 on page 108). Try variegated embroidery floss for added texture and eye appeal.

Step 8. Use brown floss to embroider the ribs on the pumpkins with the stem stitch. Embroider veins on the leaves and vines around the pumpkins using green floss and the stem stitch.

Step 9. *With wrong sides together and using a ¾-inch seam,* sew the long edge of each of the two check strips to a plaid strip. Press the seams open and trim the seam of the check strip to ⅜ inch. Turn the plaid seam allowance over the trimmed seam allowance and press. Turn under the raw edge of the wide seam allowance with the narrower seam allowance tucked inside it. The folded edge should be ⅜ inch from the stitching; press. Edgestitch to complete the flat-felled seams (Fig. 2).

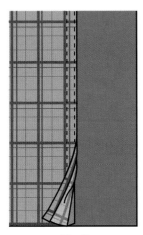

Fig. 2
Make flat-felled seams.

Step 10. Add the remaining check strip to one of the strip pairs in the same manner. Sew the two units together to complete the lower section of the banner.

Step 11. With wrong sides facing, sew the upper and lower sections of the banner together and complete the seam as described for the lower section.

Step 12. Turn under and press a narrow double hem at each short end of the 6 x 24-inch strip for the hanging sleeve. Stitch. Fold the strip in half lengthwise with wrong sides together and press. Center the folded strip on the right side of the banner with raw edges even and baste in place (Fig. 3).

Fig. 3
Baste sleeve to upper edge of banner.

Step 13. Working on a large, flat surface, pin the banner to the lining rectangle with right sides together. Make sure the lining is smooth and flat. Stitch ¾ inch from the raw edges, leaving a 6-inch-long opening in one long edge for turning. Trim the lining even with the banner raw edges.

Step 14. Turn the banner right side out through the opening and press, turning in the opening edges. Slipstitch the opening edges together.

Step 15. On the back of the banner, slipstitch the lower edge of the hanging sleeve to the lining only. ❖

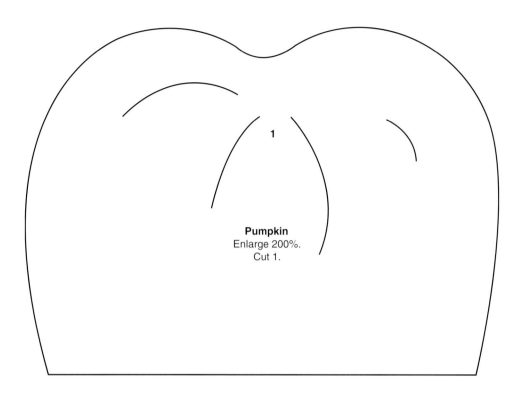

Pumpkin
Enlarge 200%.
Cut 1.

1

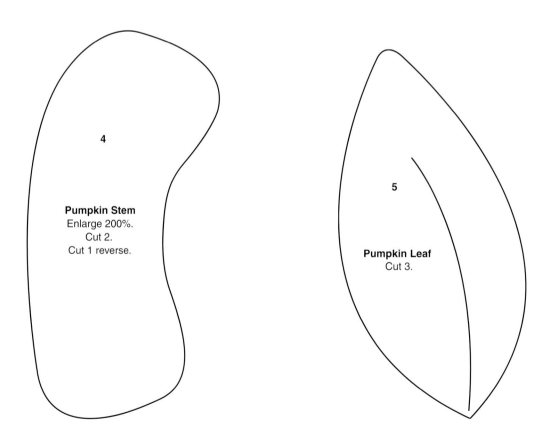

4

Pumpkin Stem
Enlarge 200%.
Cut 2.
Cut 1 reverse.

5

Pumpkin Leaf
Cut 3.

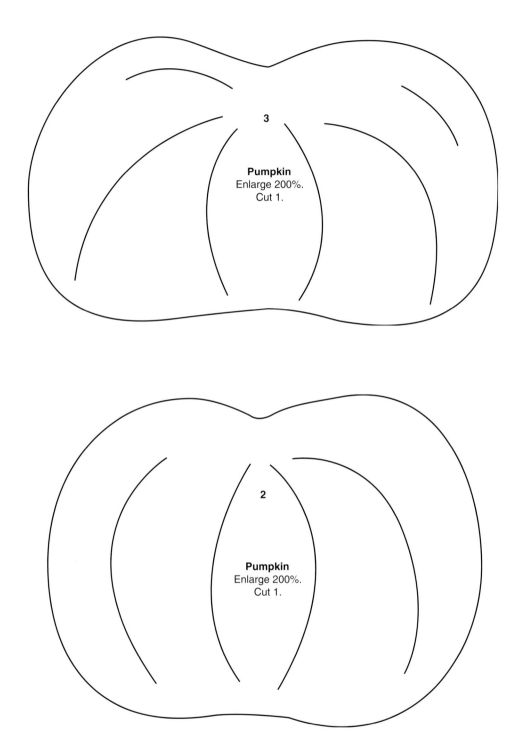

3

Pumpkin
Enlarge 200%.
Cut 1.

2

Pumpkin
Enlarge 200%.
Cut 1.

Sassy Sunflowers

Set a pretty fall table with this scalloped runner and matching place mats. Silk flowers make the matching napkin rings.

DESIGN BY JUDITH SANDSTROM

Project Specifications
Table Runner Size: 24 x 42 inches
Place Mat: 12 x 18 inches
Napkin: 17½ inches square
Napkin Ring: 1¾ inches in diameter

Materials
Table Runner
Project Note: Yardages are for 44/45-inch-wide cotton fabrics.

- 1½ yards brown/off-white print for scallops and backing
- ½ yard off-white tone-on-tone print for runner
- ½ yard tone-on-tone yellow print for flowers
- ¼ yard green tone-on-tone print for leaves
- ⅛ yard brown tone-on-tone print for flower centers
- ⅛ yard green print for border
- 1 yard lightweight paper-backed fusible web tape
- 3¼ yards ¼-inch-wide iron-on fusible web
- 18 x 36-inch piece thin cotton batting
- All-purpose thread to match appliqué fabrics

Two Place Mats & Napkins
- ¾ yard brown/off-white print for scallops and backing

- ½ yard off-white tone-on-tone print for place mat centers
- Two 8 x 14-inch pieces cotton batting
- ¼ yard or scraps of tone-on-tone prints in yellow, green and brown for appliqués
- ¾ yard green print for border and napkins
- ½ yard lightweight paper-backed fusible web
- 2½ yards ¼-inch-wide iron-on fusible web
- All-purpose thread to match appliqué fabrics

Two Napkin Rings
- 2 silk sunflowers with a 6-inch wire stem
- 2 strips of brown/off-white print, each 1½ x 30 inches
- Wire cutter

All Projects
- Rotary cutter, mat and ruler
- Template plastic
- Pen or fine-tip marker
- Small sharp scissors
- Pinking shears
- Basic sewing tools and equipment

Project Note: Wash and iron all fabrics to remove wrinkles before cutting.

Table Runner

Step 1. From the off-white print, cut a rectangle 18 x 36 inches.

Step 2. On the paper side of a 17 x 18-inch piece of fusible web, trace eight sunflowers. Leave ½ inch of space between the flowers. Apply the fusible web to the wrong side of the yellow print. Cut out the flowers along the traced lines and remove the backing paper.

Step 3. On the paper side of a 9 x 18-inch piece of fusible web, trace 16 leaves. Leave ½ inch of space between the leaves. Apply the fusible web to the wrong side of the green tone-on-tone print. Cut out the leaves and remove the backing paper.

Step 4. Trace eight flower centers onto a 4 x 17-inch strip of fusible web. Apply to the brown tone-on-tone print, cut out the flower centers and remove the backing paper.

Step 5. From the green print, cut two strips each 1½ x 36 inches, and two strips each 1½ x 18½ inches.

Step 6. Position the off-white print rectangle on top of the batting rectangle and hand baste the layers together ⅛ inch from the raw edges.

Step 7. With right sides together, fold the piece of brown/off-white print in half so that it measures 27 x 43 inches.

Step 8. With the off-white fabric face up, center the fabric/batting on the wrong side of the folded brown print fabric. Pin in place.

Step 9. Trace the ½- and ¾-circle templates on page 133 onto template plastic and cut out. Place the ¾ circle at each corner of the off-white rectangle and trace around the outer edge to mark the scallops. Place the ½ circle next to the traced corner and trace around the curved outer edge. Move the ½ circle around the entire outer edge and trace around it to complete the scalloped edge (Fig. 1). Unpin and remove the fabric/batting piece and set aside.

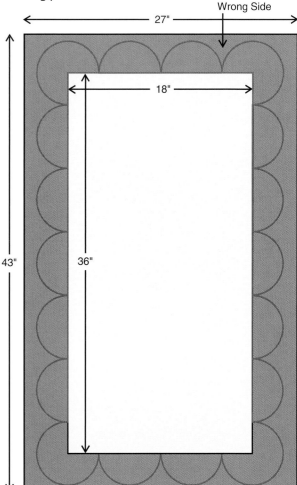

Fig. 1
Trace ½ and ¾ circles around runner center.

Step 10. Pin the two layers of the brown print together. Stitch on the traced line. Using small sharp scissors, trim the seam allowance around each curve to ¼ inch. Clip the inner points to the stitching and use pinking shears to notch out the fullness around each curve.

Step 11. Make a 6-inch-long slit in the center of one of the two brown print fabric layers. Carefully turn the piece right side out through the slit and press carefully

Step 12. Arrange the sunflowers, centers and leaves around the perimeter of the off-white print so they are at least 2 inches from the edges and about 5 inches apart. When pleased with the arrangement, fuse in place following the manufacturer's directions.

Step 13. Using thread to match the appliqués and a short, narrow zigzag setting, stitch around the outer edge of each appliqué. Pull the threads to the back of the batting, knot and trim the ends. Begin with the leaves, and then do the flowers and then the centers.

Step 14. Machine baste ½ inch from each raw edge of the layered runner and batting.

Step 15. With right sides together, pin a 1½ x 36-inch green strip to each long edge of the runner center with the raw edge along the basting. Stitch ¼ inch from the raw edges. Press the strip toward the seam allowance.

Step 16. Sew the 1½ x 18½ -inch strips to the short ends of the runner in the same manner (Fig.2).

Fig. 2
Sew borders to runner.

Step 17. Following the manufacturer's directions, apply the ¼-inch-wide fusible web tape to the right

side of each green border strip along the raw edges. Remove the backing paper.

Step 18. Center the runner on the scalloped border/backing unit, with the slit side against the batting. Turn under the raw edges of the border around the raw edges of the runner center and finger-press. Check to make sure the runner is perfectly centered on the scalloped background before fusing the border edges in place.

Step 19. Using green thread, stitch along the inner and outer edges of the green print to complete the table runner (Fig. 3).

Fig. 3
Stitch runner center to scalloped backing.

Place Mats & Napkins

Step 1. Trace four sunflowers, four centers and eight leaves on the paper side of the fusible web, leaving space between the pieces and keeping the same shapes together in one area of the paper. Cut out the pieces in groups and apply each one to the wrong side of the appropriate scrap. Cut out each shape and remove the backing paper.

Step 2. From the green print, cut two 18-inch squares for the napkins. Cut four strips each 1 x 14 inches and four strips each 1 x 9 inches.

Step 3. From the brown/off-white print, cut four pieces each 12½ x 18½ inches.

Step 4. From the off-white tone-on-tone print, cut two pieces each 8 x 14 inches.

Step 5. With right sides facing, stitch the 12½ x 18½-inch brown pieces together in pairs, stitching ¼ inch from the raw edges. Carefully make a 6-inch-long slit in one layer of each pair. Clip the corners and turn right side out through the slit. Press carefully.

Step 6. With the off-white print face up on the batting, machine baste ¼ inch from the raw edges.

Step 7. Position the sunflowers, leaves and flower centers on the off-white at opposite corners and at least ¾ inch from the raw edges. Fuse in place following manufacturer's directions. Using thread to match the appliqués and a short, narrow

zigzag, stitch around the outer edge of each motif. Pull threads to the back of the batting, knot and trim ends.

Step 8. With right sides together and raw edges even, pin a 1 x 14-inch green print strip to each long edge of the place-mat center. Stitch ¼ inch from the raw edges. Press the strips toward the seam allowances. Add the 1 x 9-inch strips to the short ends in the same manner.

Step 9. Following the manufacturer's directions, apply the ¼-inch-wide fusible web tape to the right side of each green border strip along the raw edges. Remove the backing paper. Turn under the raw edge and finger-press in place.

Step 10. Center the place mat center on the slit side of the brown rectangle. When perfectly aligned, fuse in place.

Step 11. Using green thread, stitch along the inner and outer edges of the green borders to complete the place-mat.

Step 12. Make narrow double hems along each edge of each napkin.

Napkin Ring

Step 1. Turn under and press ¼ inch along each raw edge of the 1½ x 30-inch fabric strip. Fold in half lengthwise with turned edges aligned and edgestitch to make a finished ½-inch-wide band.

Step 2. If the silk sunflower has leaves, slide them up the stem so they are close to the flower.

Step 3. Bend the wire stem into a 1¾-inch-diameter circle and twist the wire ends around themselves twice to secure. Trim off excess with the wire cutter.

Step 4. Leaving a 6-inch-long section of the brown print band free and beginning at the underside of the flower, wind the band tightly around the curved stem, overlapping at ¼-inch intervals or less.

Step 5. Tie the band ends together in a bow to complete the napkin ring. ❖

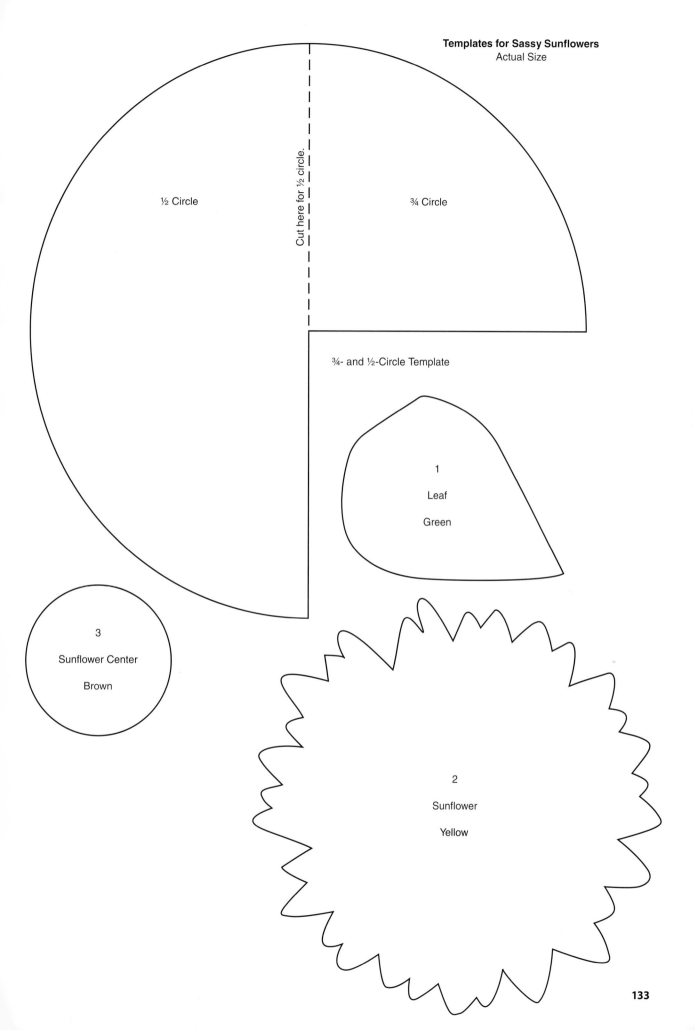

½ Circle

Cut here for ½ circle.

¾ Circle

¾- and ½-Circle Template

1

Leaf

Green

3

Sunflower Center

Brown

2

Sunflower

Yellow

Tabletop Elegance

Make a pretty pieced table topper to suit any season or decor. Beautiful for a formal table, the featured cloth is made of silk and silklike fabrics, trimmed with organza ribbon and brush fringe and backed with a silky fabric. For a more casual approach, use the same technique with cotton fabrics and grosgrain ribbon.

DESIGN BY CAROL ZENTGRAF

Project Specifications

Table Cover Size: 53 inches square, excluding fringe

Materials

Project Note: *Yardages are for 54-inch-wide decorator silk and silklike fabrics.*

- ½ yard each: 3 gold and 3 red fabrics for patches
- 1⅝ yards gold or red for backing
- Two 20-yard spools ⅝-wide organza ribbon
- 6¼ yards tassel trim
- Permanent fabric adhesive
- Rotary cutter, mat and ruler
- All-purpose thread to match fabrics and ribbon
- Basic sewing tools and equipment

Instructions

Project Note: *Use ½-inch-wide seam allowances and stitch all seams with right sides together.*

Step 1. Using rotary-cutting tools, cut 28 red pieces and 21 gold pieces each 9 inches square. From the backing fabric, cut a 54-inch square.

Step 2. Arrange the squares in four rows of red and three rows of gold. Sew the squares together in each row and press the seams open (Fig. 1).

Step 3. With the seams aligned, sew the rows together, alternating red and gold rows. Press the seams open.

Step 4. Center and sew a doubled layer of organza ribbon over each seam line, stitching close to both edges of the ribbon.

Step 5. Trim the edges of the pieced topper as needed so that it is 54 inches square.

Step 6. With right sides together, sew the patchwork piece to the backing square, leaving an 8-inch-long opening in one edge for turning. Turn right side out and press. Slipstitch the opening closed.

Step 7. Use permanent fabric adhesive to adhere the trim to the edges of the topper. Turn the end under where it meets the beginning of the trim and glue in place. ❖

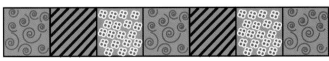

Make 4.

Make 3.

Fig. 1
Arrange squares in rows
and sew together.

Winter
Wonders

Sew something cozy to warm the wintry days ahead, or get a jump on the holidays with festive Christmas projects designed to tickle your fancy and decorate your home.

Let It Snow!

Take a simple vest or jacket pattern and add seasonal appliqués, chenille trim and polymer clay buttons for a mother-daughter duo that's sure to keep them warm and garner admiring glances from onlookers.

DESIGN BY CAROL ZENTGRAF

Project Specifications
Jacket and Vest Sizes: Sized to fit

Materials for Vest or Jacket
- Simple jacket or vest pattern with button closure of your choice
- Knit fleece fabric in yardage given on pattern envelope for chosen size
- ⅓ yard cotton print for facings
- 5 x 7-inch rectangle white tone-on-tone print
- 2 (5-inch) squares green plaid for the jacket or 1 square for the vest
- Scraps of a snowflake print
- Chenille By The Inch in white, green, blue and brown
- Chenille By The Inch cutting guide and chenille brush
- ½-inch-diameter button forms for covered buttons: 5 for jacket; 4 for vest
- Polymer-clay buttons:
    - 2 carrot nose
    - 4 mittens
    - 4 holly leaves
    - 8 tiny snowflakes
- All-purpose thread to match fabrics
- Paper-backed fusible web (double-stick recommended)
- Tear-away stabilizer
- Water-soluble stabilizer
- Rotary cutter and mat
- Water-filled spray bottle
- Press cloth

Instructions

Step 1. Follow the pattern guidesheet to make the jacket or vest from fleece. Use water-soluble stabilizer on top of the garment when making the buttonholes. Tear away the excess; what is trapped under the stitches will dissolve in the wash.

Step 2. Cover the buttons with scraps of the snowflake print, centering a snowflake on each button. Sew the buttons in place.

Step 3. Trace the appliqué templates on pages 140 and 141 onto the paper backing of the fusible web, tracing two trees for the jacket, one for the child's vest. Cut out each shape leaving a ¼-inch-wide margin beyond the drawn lines.

Step 4. Fuse the snowman to the wrong side of the white print and the trees to the wrong side of the green plaid fabric. Cut out the shapes. Remove the paper backing and position the pieces on the jacket or vest front, referring to the photos for placement. Using a press cloth, fuse the pieces in place; do not touch a hot iron directly to the fleece fabric. It will melt!

Step 5. Adjust your sewing machine for a blanket stitch and stitch around the outer edge of each appliqué. If you prefer, you can do the blanket stitching by hand (see illustrations on page 108). It will just take a little longer.

Step 6. Cut pieces of stabilizer large enough to cover each tree and the snowman, and cut three 4-inch squares for the snowflakes. Trace the garland placement lines onto the pieces for the trees, the scarf and arms onto the piece for the snowman, and a snowflake onto each snowflake square. Pin the appropriate pieces over the trees and snowman. Refer to the photo and pin the snowflake pieces in place. If desired, add random stabilizer strips to make snow on the ground.

Step 7. Follow the manufacturer's directions to remove the backing from the chenille and to cut the required strips. Cut green strips to fit the garland lines, brown to fit the snowman arms, blue to fit the scarf and white to fit the snowflakes. Position the chenille strips on the appliqués and stitch in place along the center stitching lines of the strips; do not remove the stabilizer. Spray the strips lightly with water and use the chenille brush to make the strips fray up to the stitching lines. Allow the strips to dry, and then remove the stabilizer.

Step 8. Referring to the photo, hand sew the polymer-clay buttons in place. ❖

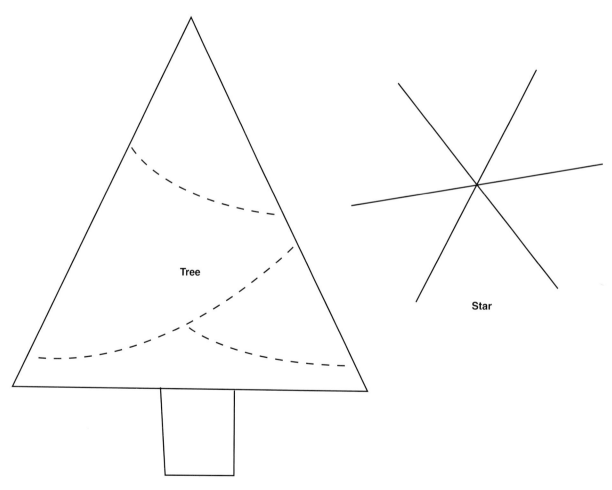

Templates for Let It Snow
Actual Size

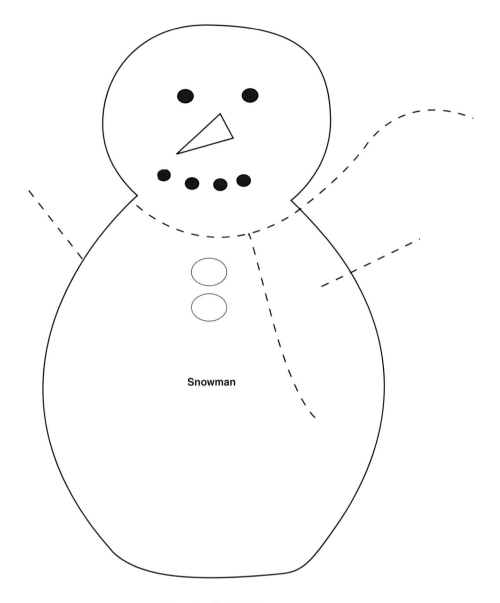

Snowman

Template for Let It Snow
Actual Size

Make It Yours

Use these appliqués to design your own fleece pillows, or stockings to hang by the fireplace with care. Knit fleece doesn't ravel so you can cut simple squares to fit the pillow form, adding 1 inch all around for seam allowances. Then sew the pieces together with wrong sides facing. Use your pinking shears or a wavy blade on your rotary cutter to trim the seam edges for an instant finish. You can do the same with stockings. Use the stocking patterns provided for other projects in this book or draw your own in the desired size.

Christmas in the Neighborhood

Hang this snowy scene above your mantel for the holiday season and enjoy the snow without weathering the cold.

DESIGN BY EILEEN WESTFALL

Project Specifications

Quilt Size: 25 x 44 inches

Materials

Project Note: Yardages are given for 44/45-inch-wide cotton fabric.

- ½ yard dark blue print for sky
- ¼ yard white tone-on-tone print for the snow
- ¼ yard red print for appliqués and inner border
- ½ yard dark green print for outer border
- 1⅜ yards print for backing
- ⅓ yard red print for binding
- Assorted scraps blue, green, beige, red and yellow prints
- Scrap of black fabric
- Paper-backed fusible web (optional)
- 1 yard ¹⁄₁₆-inch-wide red satin ribbon
- 10 small heart buttons
- 1 skein each of black, red, yellow, brown and green 6-strand embroidery floss
- 26 x 46-inch piece lightweight batting
- Rotary cutter, mat and ruler
- Template plastic
- All-purpose thread to match fabric
- Quilting needles and thread for hand quilting (optional)
- Basic sewing tools and equipment

Instructions

Project Notes: Use ¼-inch-wide seam allowances for piecing the background and house blocks.

Finished house blocks have a ¼-inch-wide turn-under allowance along the side and lower edges. All other appliqué templates do not have turn-under allowances. You will need to add them for needle-turn appliqué.

For faster fusible appliqué with raw edges, cut the shapes from fabrics backed with paper-backed fusible web (see below) and fuse them in place following the manufacturer's directions.

Step 1. Refer to Fig. 1 for Steps 1–3. From the blue print, cut one 12 x 35-inch rectangle. From the white print, cut one strip 4½ x 35 inches. With right sides together, stitch the white strip to one long edge of the blue rectangle and press the seam toward the blue panel.

Step 2. From the red print, cut two strips each 2 x 16 inches for the inner side borders. Sew the strips to the

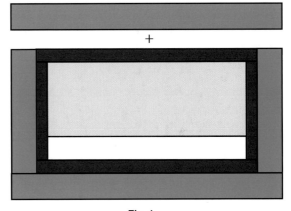

Fig. 1
Patchwork Panel Assembly

short edges of the panel from Step 1 and press the seams toward the borders. Cut two strips each 2 x 38 inches. Sew the strips to the top and bottom edges of the panel and press the seams toward the borders.

Step 3. From the green print, cut two strips each 3½ x 19 inches and two strips each 3½ x 44 inches. Sew to the panel from Step 2, adding the side borders first, followed by the top and bottom borders. Press the seams toward the green borders. Set the patchwork panel aside while you cut and prepare the appliqués.

Step 4. From the beige print for one house, cut two 1½ x 3½-inch rectangles (A), one 2½ x 4½-inch rectangle (C) and two 2½ x 5½-inch rectangles (D). Trace the roof template (E) on page 145 onto template plastic and cut out. Trace around the template and cut one and one reversed from the beige print fabric. For the door (B), cut one 2½ x 3½-inch rectangle from a green print. Repeat the above to cut the pieces for a second beige house from the same or a different beige fabric.

Step 5. Refer to Step 4 to cut the pieces for a green house. Cut the roof from a green print. Cut the door from a beige print.

Step 6. Arrange the pieces for each house as shown in Fig. 2 and sew together. Press the seams as directed by the arrows. Turn under and press ¼ inch on the side and bottom edges of each house to prepare them for appliqué.

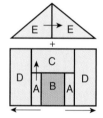

Fig. 2
House Block Assembly
Make 2 beige houses and 1 green house.
Press in direction of arrows.

Step 7. From yellow print, cut nine 1-inch squares for the large windows.

Step 8. Cut the required number of each appliqué piece (templates on pages 146 and 147) from the appropriate-color fabric. For needle-turn appliqué, cut out each piece with a ¼-inch-wide turn-under allowance beyond the shape. For fusible appliqué, apply paper-backed fusible web to the wrong side of the fabric scraps. Draw the shapes onto the paper and cut out on the marked lines. Remove the paper backing, position as directed and fuse in place.

Step 9. Fold the patchwork panel in half vertically to locate the center and mark with a pin. Repeat with the green house. Center the house on the patchwork panel with the lower edge slightly overlapping the snow/sky seam. Position a beige house to each side of the green house with 2¾ inches of space between them. Appliqué the folded edges in place.

Step 10. Referring to the detail photos of the houses, position the windows and windows with dormers on the houses and appliqué in place. Embroider the window details with 2 strands of black embroidery floss and the outline (stem) stitch. Appliqué a doormat to the snow below each door. Embroider a doorknob using the satin stitch or make a French knot for each one. Embroider a light at the upper right-hand side of the door using black and yellow floss. Refer to quilt photo.

Step 11. From a red print for the roof eaves, cut four strips each ⅝ x 6 inches. Cut two strips from a contrasting green print for the green house. Referring to Fig. 3 and the detail photos, position and appliqué the smoke, chimney and eaves in numerical order.

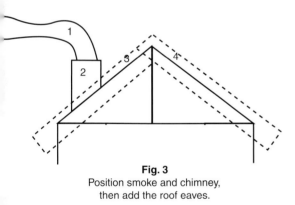

Fig. 3
Position smoke and chimney,
then add the roof eaves.

Step 12. Referring to the detail photos, position the trees, snowman and street lamp appliqués. Follow the numerical order for each one. Appliqué in place and add embroidered details.

Step 13. For the hat brim on the snowman, embroider along the lower edge and a few stitches past the head on each side. Use the outline stitch. Embroider stick arms on the snowman and satin-stitch buttons down the front of him—or substitute tiny black buttons. Make French knots for the eyes and nose, and use the outline stitch to embroider the mouth.

Step 14. Make three small bows from the narrow red ribbon and tack one in place at the top of each wreath. Sew five heart buttons to each wreath, positioning each on an X.

Step 15. For each holiday greeting sign, cut a 1½ x 3-inch piece of light print. Position over the full-size patterns on page 147 and trace the letters and holiday motifs. Embroider as directed. Turn under and press ¼ inch all around each piece. Position a greeting on each house and sew in place.

Step 16. From the backing fabric, cut a 26 x 46-inch piece. Layer the completed quilt top with the batting and backing. Hand- or pin-baste the layers together. Quilt as desired by hand or machine and remove the basting.

Step 17. Trim the batting and backing even with the quilt-top edges.

Step 18. From the binding fabric, cut four 2½-inch-wide strips for double-layer binding. Bind the edges using your favorite binding method. ❖

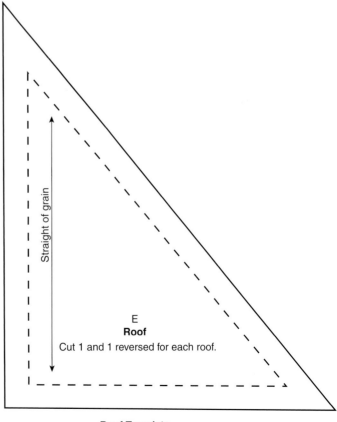

Straight of grain

E
Roof
Cut 1 and 1 reversed for each roof.

Roof Template
Actual Size

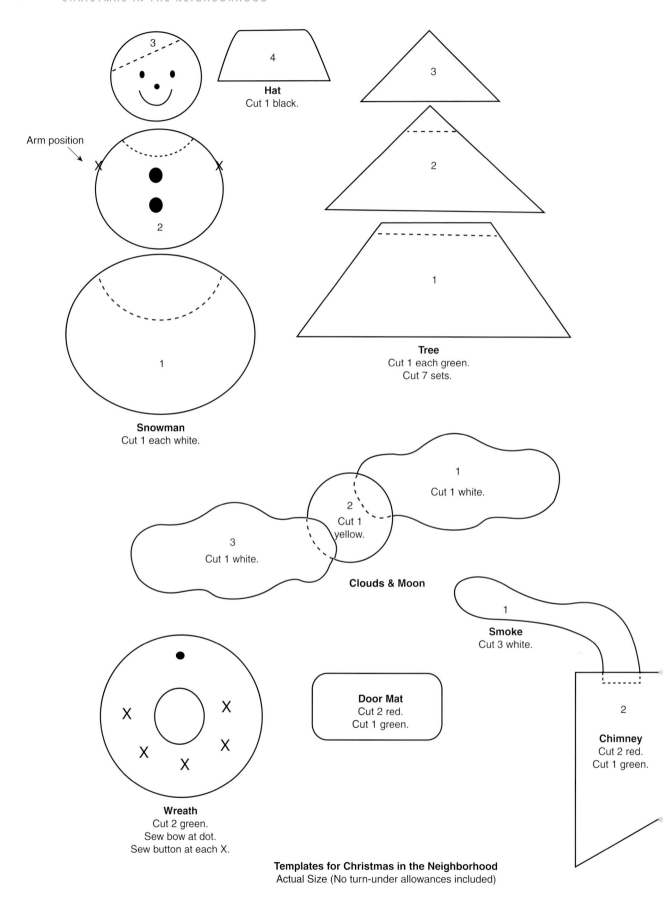

Hat
Cut 1 black.

Tree
Cut 1 each green.
Cut 7 sets.

Arm position

Snowman
Cut 1 each white.

Clouds & Moon

3
Cut 1 white.

2
Cut 1
yellow.

1
Cut 1 white.

Smoke
Cut 3 white.

Door Mat
Cut 2 red.
Cut 1 green.

Chimney
Cut 2 red.
Cut 1 green.

Wreath
Cut 2 green.
Sew bow at dot.
Sew button at each X.

Templates for Christmas in the Neighborhood
Actual Size (No turn-under allowances included)

Templates for Christmas in the Neighborhood
Actual Size (No turn-under allowance included)

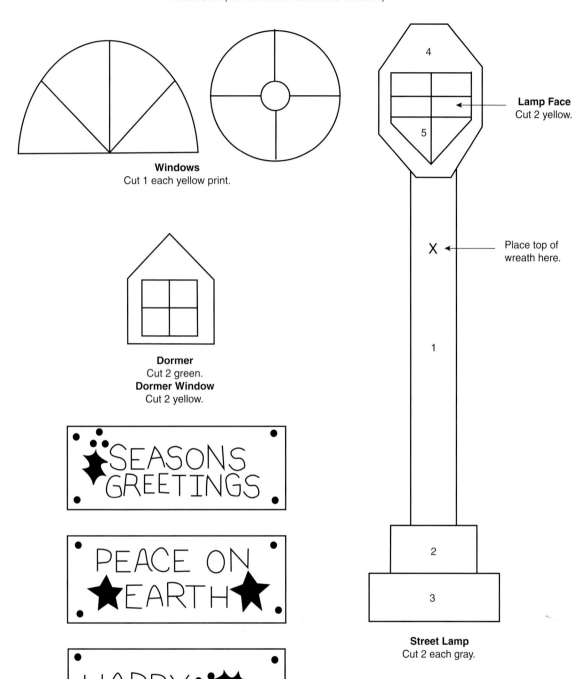

Windows
Cut 1 each yellow print.

Dormer
Cut 2 green.
Dormer Window
Cut 2 yellow.

Lamp Face
Cut 2 yellow.

Place top of
wreath here.

Street Lamp
Cut 2 each gray.

Signs
Finished sign size: 1 x 2½",
seam allowance not included.
Backstitch lettering, satin-stitch
holly leaves and stars. Work French
knots for holly berries and at corners.

Think Snow

Rhinestone-studded snowflakes on this frosty welcome banner greet your guests with a wintry salutation.

DESIGN BY ANNABELLE KELLER

Project Specifications

Banner Size: 19 x 33 inches

Materials

Project Note: Yardage given for 44/45-inch-wide cotton fabric.

- ¼ yard white tone-on-tone print
- ¼ yard white solid
- 1 yard dark blue tone-on-tone print
- 1 yard medium blue tone-on-tone print
- 1 yard lightweight paper-backed fusible web
- 1 yard tear-away stabilizer
- 1⅓ yards ¼-inch-diameter metallic silver twisted cord with cut ends taped
- 2 (3-inch-long) silver metallic tassels
- 22 x 36-inch piece fusible batting
- All-purpose threads to match fabrics
- Rotary cutter, mat and ruler
- 2 wooden ball knobs, 1 inch in diameter with ½-inch-diameter holes
- 20¾-inch-long piece of ½-inch-diameter dowel
- Silver metallic spray paint
- Fine silver braid
- Silver permanent glitter spray
- 1 package each of the following rhinestones style and sizes: 13 x 8mm drops and 5mm round for Snowflake A; 7mm and 10mm round for Snowflake B; 5mm and 10mm round and 15 x 7mm navettes for Snowflake C
- Fabric, wood and jewel glues
- Open-toe presser foot and metallic needle for sewing machine
- Basic sewing tools and equipment

Instructions

Project Notes: Use ¼-inch-wide seam allowances. Wash, dry and press all fabrics.

Step 1. Following the directions on the can, apply silver metallic spray paint to the wooden balls and dowel. Allow to dry.

Step 2. Apply fusible web to the wrong side of the white tone-on-tone print fabric following manufacturer's directions. Remove the paper and fuse the print fabric to the piece of white soild fabric.

Step 3. Trace the letters (2 Ns and 1 each of the remaining letters) on page 152 onto the paper side of the remaining fusible web. Leave ½ inch of space between shapes as you trace. Enlarge the snowflake patterns on page 151 and trace around each one on the paper side of the fusible web. Cut out the letters and snowflakes with a ¼-inch-wide margin around the outer edges of each shape.

Step 4. Apply the fusible-web letters and snowflakes to the white solid fabric of the fused fabric from step 2. Cut out each shape on the traced lines.

Step 5. From the dark blue print, cut one 6 x 30½-inch strip along the lengthwise grain for the THINK SNOW background, three 9½-inch squares for the snowflake blocks and three 2½ x 40-inch strips for the binding.

Step 6. From the medium blue print, cut one 2 x 30½-inch lattice strip along the lengthwise grain and two 2 x 9½-inch lattice strips. For the borders, cut two 2 x 16½-inch strips and two 2 x

33½-inch strips. For the backing, cut one 22 x 36-inch rectangle. For the hanging sleeve, cut one 5 x 19-inch strip.

Step 7. Remove the paper backing on the snowflakes. Center each one on the right side of a 9½-inch blue block and fuse in place following the manufacturer's directions.

Step 8. Remove the backing paper and arrange the THINK SNOW letters on the long blue panel. Fuse in place. Apply a light coat of fabric glitter spray to the snowflakes. Allow to dry.

Step 9. Place tear-away stabilizer on the wrong side of each block and the long panel with the lettering. Adjust the machine for a narrow satin stitch and thread the needle with silver metallic thread. Satin stitch over the raw edges of the appliqués. Tear away the stabilizer carefully to avoid distorting the stitches.

Step 10. Arrange the banner pieces as shown in Fig. 1 and sew together. Press the seams as directed by the arrows.

Fig. 1
Banner Assembly

Step 11. Place the 22 x 36-inch backing rectangle face down on a large, flat surface. Center and smooth the fusible batting in place on top. Place the quilt top face up on top of the batting. The batting and backing will extend beyond the quilt-top edges. Following the manufacturer's instructions, fuse the layers together, taking care not to touch the batting with the iron.

Step 12. Quilt as desired. Trim the batting and backing even with the quilt top.

Step 13. Sew the binding strips together with bias seams to make one long strip. Press the seams open. Fold the strip in half lengthwise with wrong sides together and press. Bind the quilt, beginning close to the center on one long edge and mitering the corners as you reach them. Turn the folded edge of the binding over the raw edge to the back of the quilt and slipstitch in place, mitering the corners as you reach them.

Step 14. Make a double narrow hem at each short end of the 5 x 19-inch medium blue for the hanging sleeve. Fold the strip in half lengthwise with wrong sides together and stitch ¼ inch from the raw edges. Center the seam on the back of the tube and press the seam open. Press both long folded edges to crease.

Step 15. Position one creased edge 1½ inches below the upper edge on the back of the banner; pin. Slipstitch in place. (Refer to Fig. 4 for Sailing Through Summer on page 53). Pin the lower edge of the tube in place ½ inch above and parallel to the folded edge. Turn the tube back against the pins and slipstitch in place, taking care to catch only the underlayer of the tube to the banner. Remove the pins. This method creates slack in the upper layer of the hanging sleeve to accommodate the hanging rod.

Step 16. Insert the silver dowel through the hanging sleeve. Glue ball knobs to the dowel ends. Measure 8 inches from each end of the metallic cord and knot once around the dowel next to the knob at each end. Glue the cord knot to the dowel. Knot each end of the cord ¾ inch from each end. Apply glue to the knots and untwist the cord below the knots.

Step 17. Remove the hanging loop cord from the tassels. Place each tassel top ½ inch from the taped end of the cord and glue in place. Use fine silver braid to wrap and tie the tassel. Glue the braid in place to begin, and then wrap about ¾ inch of the tassel. Glue the end of the braid in place.

Step 18. Referring to the snowflake templates, arrange rhinestones on the snowflakes and glue in place with jewel glue. Allow to dry. ❖

Snowflake C Template
Enlarge 200%

Rhinestones:
large round (10mm)
small round (5mm)
15 x 7mm navettes

Snowflake A Template
Enlarge 200%

Rhinestones:
13 x 8mm drops
5mm round

Snowflake B Template
Enlarge 200%

Rhinestones:
small round (7mm)
large round (10mm)

Templates for Think Snow
Actual Size

Dance With Me Evening Bag

Convert fabric from a retired evening dress and the velvet collar from an outdated shirt to make this romantic little purse. The clutch is just large enough to hold your dance card and lipstick for holiday parties. Embellish it with a dramatic brooch or a collection of antique buttons.

DESIGN BY LUCY B. GRAY

Project Specifications

Evening Bag Size: 6 x 10 inches

Materials

- Dressy shirt with a collar that has a separate band
- Fabric from another dressy blouse or shirt or ⅓ yard light-to medium-weight dressy fabric
- ⅓ yard polyester fleece
- ⅓ yard muslin (optional, for sample)
- Pattern tracing paper or cloth for pattern
- Permanent marker
- Embellishments (antique buttons, beads, pearls from an old necklace, costume jewelry pieces)
- All-purpose thread to match fabrics
- Basic sewing tools and equipment

Instructions

Step 1. Cut the collar and band from the shirt below the finished band edge, taking care not to cut into the band itself. Use a seam ripper to remove all the stitching along the lower edge of the band and remove all loose fabric and threads. Carefully remove the buttonhole stitching and the button, making it possible to reattach the collar and band to the upper edge of the handbag. Hand baste the seam allowances to the individual collar bands so the lower edges of the band are folded along the original seam line.

Step 2. Cut the seams free from a dressy shirt or skirt or use coordinating fabric for the bag. There's enough "yardage" in the upper sleeves or the back of a shirt for the two pieces of the bag body.

Step 3. Cut a 6 x 14-inch piece of pattern tracing paper or cloth and fold in half crosswise. Round the corners to make the bag pattern (Fig. 1).

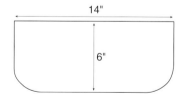

Fig. 1
Make bag pattern.

Step 4. Use the pattern to cut two bag pieces from the outer bag fabric and from the lining fabric. If the outer fabric is not completely opaque, underline it with a lightweight woven fabric in a color that matches or coordinates so the fleece interlining won't show through.

Project Note: *Underlining adds stability and body to lightweight fabric such as the velvet-flocked silk in the bag shown in the photo.*

Step 5. Serge- or zigzag-finish the raw edges of each piece.

Step 6. With right sides facing, pin and stitch the bag pieces together using a ⅜-inch-wide seam allowance. Turn right side out. Repeat with the bag lining pieces but use a ½-inch-wide seam allowance so the lining will fit smoothly inside the bag. *Do not turn right side out.* Finger-press the seams open on the bag and lining at the side edges.

Step 7. Machine baste ¼ inch from the upper edge of the lining. Repeat with the bag. Tuck the lining inside the bag. Draw up the bobbin threads on both layers to fit the lower edge of the collar band when it is pinned closed (Fig. 2).

Fig. 2
Draw up bobbin threads to gather upper edge.

Step 8. Remove the lining and place the gathered shape on the polyester fleece. Trace around it with the permanent marker, taking care not to mark on the lining (Fig 3). Trace a second bag shape. Remove the lining and cut the fleece shapes on the marked line.

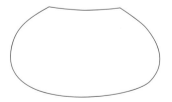

Fig. 3
Cut 2 from fleece.

Step 9. Place the fleece pieces inside the bag against the front and back, and make sure they lie smooth and flat inside.

Step 10. Replace the lining so the fleece pieces lie between the bag and the lining on each side. Pin the upper edges together all the way around, making sure that the lining and bag side seams are aligned. Adjust the gathers evenly.

Step 11. Machine baste along the lower edge of the inner collar band and draw up the bobbin thread to gather slightly. Place the lower edge of the gathered band over the bag raw edges so the lining, bag and batting layers are encased between the two layers of the collar and the band ends overlap at the center front. Adjust the fit of the band to the bag edge, adjusting the gathers as needed. Tie off the threads to secure the gathers in the lining, bag and band edge.

Step 12. Remove the collar and band from the bag and hand baste the upper edges of the bag together ¼ inch from the raw edges.

Step 13. Replace the collar and band, and pin in place with the bag edges tucked as far as possible into the collar band. Make sure that the band ends overlap at the center front of the bag, with the buttonhole end underneath to hide it. Using small hidden stitches, sew the lower edge of the band to the outside of the bag.

Step 14. Turn the inner band away from the outer band, lap the loose front ends and sew them together neatly. Sew the lower edge of the inner band to the lining with small, discreet stitches.

Step 15. Sew vintage buttons in complementary colors to the bag front where the collar points meet. ❖

Embellish Your Bag

Embellishments for your bag can take any form. You can stitch beads or sequins to the bag fabric, attach glittery charms made from old earrings, or recycle the pearls from a necklace that needs restringing. Let the colors of the collar and bag fabric guide you. If the fabric has cool tones (blues, grays), use silver-based jewelry accents and trims. With warm-toned fabrics (reds, browns), go with gold or bronze metallic accents. Warm with warm, cool with cool!

Check out antique and secondhand shops for mother-of-pearl buttons that contribute a vintage, romantic feel. Sprinkle them over the bag's surface or center one or two in a row beneath the collar, like a shirt front.

Crazy for Quilting

Create these festive holiday pillows using an easy flip-and-stitch crazy-quilting technique and scraps of favorite fabrics and trims. You can use the same pattern shape and technique to make coordinating holiday stockings if you wish.

DESIGN BY CAROL ZENTGRAF

Project Specifications
Stocking Pillow Size: 13 x 19 inches
Tree Pillow Size: 15 x 20 inches

Materials for Each Pillow
- Assorted scraps coordinating fabrics each 4 inches square or larger
- 16 x 21-inch rectangle of fabric for pillow back
- 16 x 21-inch rectangle of muslin
- ⅓ yard each of 2 or 3 coordinating trims
- Pattern tracing cloth or paper
- Polyester fiberfill
- Self-adhesive basting tape (optional)
- Fabric marker
- Rotary cutter, mat and ruler
- All-purpose sewing thread to match fabrics
- Pinking shears
- Basic sewing tools and equipment

Instructions
Project Note: *The assembly is the same for both pillow shapes. Use rotary-cutting equipment to cut the scraps into irregular geometric shapes as you work. Use ¼-inch-wide seam allowances.*

Step 1. Enlarge the patterns (Figs. 1 and 2 on page 158) on pattern tracing cloth or paper. Trace the chosen pillow shape (tree or stocking) onto the muslin.

Step 2. Place the muslin on the wrong side of the backing fabric and cut the tree or stocking from both fabrics. Set the backing aside.

Step 3. Refer to Fig. 3 for Steps 3–6. Numbers in parentheses refer to the order for adding crazy patches. Choose a fabric for the center of the pillow (piece 1) and position on the muslin shape. Machine stitch a scant ¼ inch from all edges.

Step 4. Measure one edge of the shape and cut another irregularly shaped geometric patch (piece 2) from a different fabric with one edge a bit longer than the edge you measured. Pin it to the first piece with right sides together and the raw edges aligned. Stitch ¼ inch from the aligned edges. Flip the second piece onto the muslin and press. Pin the shapes to the muslin to keep them in place or use basting tape to adhere the unstitched edges to the muslin. It will not be removed.

Note: *If you wish, you can use a ruler and pen to preplan the arrangement on the muslin. Draw the center shape first and then draw the varying shapes around the center, always working in one direction around the center.*

Step 5. Measure the edge of the patchwork. Cut and add another strip as described in Step 4. Flip, press and pin.

Step 6. Continue in this fashion until the entire piece of muslin is covered with crazy patchwork. The patchwork pieces should completely cover the muslin shape with excess fabric extending past the cut edges.

Step 7. With the muslin side up, baste around the edges to secure the patchwork to the muslin. Trim the patchwork even with the muslin edges.

Step 8. Use basting tape to adhere trim to some of the seam lines as desired. Stitch in place.

Step 9. With right sides together, sew the pillow backing to the patchwork and leave a 4-inch-long opening in the lower edge for turning. Clip the inward corners and across outward corners on the tree. Use pinking shears to notch out fullness in the curved edges of the stocking pillow. Turn right side out and press. Turn in the edges of the opening and press.

Step 10. Stuff the pillow with fiberfill to the desired fullness. Slipstitch the opening closed. ❖

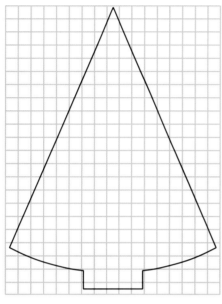

Fig.1
Tree Pillow Pattern
1 square = 1"

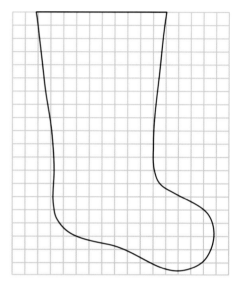

Fig. 2
Stocking Pillow Pattern
1 square = 1"

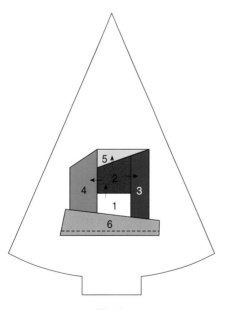

Fig. 3
Add pieces and flip onto muslin pattern.

Mix It Up

Choosing fabrics for crazy quilting is fun and easy when you follow these tips:

• Choose a focal fabric with several colors as a starting point. For example, the red plaid used in the center of the tree pillow features red, green, gold, dark green and black. Select other fabrics in these colors to mix with the focal fabric.

• Vary the fabric motifs, mixing plaids, stripes, florals and prints that are similar in scale.

• Use a variety of textures, such as the featured velvet, brocade and metallic fabrics. This provides tactile and visual interest in the finished piece

Organza
Surprises

This little organza bag holds a beaded treasure. Make several now to give as holiday keepsakes or to hang on your Christmas tree. Wear the holly pin on your lapel to dress up your winter attire.

DESIGN BY DIANA S. STUNELL-DUNSMORE

Project Specifications
Holly Leaf Bag Size: 4 x 5 inches
Dove Size: 2 x 2 inches

Materials
Holly Leaf Bag With Dove
- Scraps of dark green and red shimmer organza
- Scraps of lightweight white bridal satin
- 24-inch piece ½-inch-wide white ribbon with red edging
- Dressmaker's pencil
- 3 clear green seed beads
- 25 opalescent bugle beads
- 2 clear yellow seed beads
- 1 dark pewter seed bead
- 5 clear red seed beads
- Approximately 80 silver-lined crystal seed beads
- 6 silver-lined crystal beads about twice the size of the seed beads

Holly Pin
- Scrap of dark green and red metallic shimmer organza
- Scrap of red-and-green cotton plaid with metallic accents
- 1-inch stainless steel safety pin (not brass)

- Christmas confetti (optional)
- 5 clear red seed beads
- 10 silver-lined crystal seed beads
- 10 silver-lined crystal beads about twice the size of seed beads

Both Items

- All-purpose threads to match all fabrics
- Small amount of polyester fiberfill
- Plastic point turner
- Pinking shears
- Basic sewing tools and equipment

Instructions
Holly Leaf Bag With Dove

Step 1. Trace the dove pattern on page 163 onto the wrong side at one end of a 3 x 5-inch scrap of bridal satin. Fold the bridal-satin scrap in half with right sides together and place a straight pin through the center. Stitch on the drawn line, leaving an opening for turning along the wing upper edge.

Step 2. Trim the seam to ⅛ inch and clip curves to the stitching. Turn right side out.

Step 3. Lightly draw the wing, tail and eye markings on the front of the dove. Stuff the dove with bits of fiberfill until full but not overly plump. Slipstitch the opening closed.

Step 4. Using white thread, hand sew beads to one side of the dove around the outer edge as shown in

Fig. 1. Secure each bead with two stitches. For the beak, string two yellow beads together and tack to the outer edge and close to the dove's body. For the olive branch, tightly string three green beads together; tack to the outer edge of the dove under the beak at both ends of the string of beads. Use one pewter seed bead for the eye.

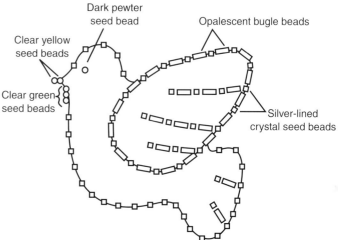

Fig. 1
Hand stitch beads as shown.

Step 5. From dark green organza, cut two holly leaf shapes using the pattern on page 163. With right sides together, stitch ¼ inch from the raw edges, leaving the upper edge open. Trim the seams to ⅛ inch, clip the curves and trim the points. Turn right side out and press lightly as needed.

Step 6. At the bottom point of the holly leaf, attach green thread and make a string of beads as shown in Fig. 2. After adding the red and crystal seed beads, bring the needle and thread around the outside of the

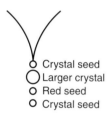

Fig. 2
String beads as shown.

last bead and insert the needle back into the string of the remaining beads. Take several small stitches in the point to secure the beads. Referring to Fig. 3, make and attach beads to the remaining points in the same manner.

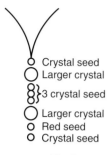

Fig. 3
String beads as shown.

Step 7. Insert the dove inside the bag; fold the raw edges under ¼ inch and press lightly. Hand baste through both turned edges close to the edge. Draw up the stitches to gather and close the bag; take several stitches to secure.

Step 8. From the red organza, cut four holly berries using the pattern on page 162. Layer the circles in pairs and use a needle with doubled thread to baste ⅛ inch from the outer edge. Place a bit of fiberfill in the center and draw up the stitches to form a ¾-inch-diameter berry. Take several stitches on the back of the berry. Repeat for the second berry.

Step 9. Sew the berries to the front of the holly leaf bag, covering the gathered edge.

Step 10. Fold the 24-inch piece of white ribbon in half and sew the fold to the back of the bag behind the berries. Use the ribbon to tie the bag to a wreath, package or tree limb.

Holly Pin

Step 1. Using the pattern on page 163, cut two holly leaves each from green organza and from the plaid fabric.

Step 2. With right sides together, stitch the leaves together in pairs ¼ inch from the raw edges. Leave the straight edge open on each leaf. Trim the seam allowances to ⅛ inch. Clip the curves and trim across the points.

Step 3. Turn the leaves right side out and use the point turner to gently poke out the points. Press lightly as needed.

Step 4. Using a single strand of dark green thread, sew beads to each point of the plaid leaf as shown in Fig. 4. Insert the needle at the point and thread the beads on the needle. After adding the last bead, bring the thread around the side of the bead and insert the needle through the first bead. Tack to the point with several tiny stitches.

Fig. 4
String beads as shown.

Step 5. Sew beads to the points of the green organza leaf in the same manner, arranging them as shown in Fig. 5.

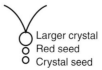

Fig. 5
String beads as shown.

Step 6. *Optional:* *Drop some Christmas confetti into the green organza leaf.* Turn under and press ¼ inch at the open end of the green and plaid leaves. Hand baste the edges together on each leaf, and then draw up the stitches to gather and close each one. Take a few stitches to secure. Tack the two leaves together with whipstitching at the gathered edges.

Step 7. Using the pattern at bottom of page , cut two circles from the red organza. Sew the circles together ⅛ inch from the raw edges. Place a small, firm ball of fiberfill in the center and draw up the stitches tightly to form a berry. Take several stitches in place to secure the gathers, and then use the remaining thread to sew the berry to the leaves to cover the area where they are tacked together.

Step 8. Sew the safety pin to the back of the holly leaves (Fig. 6). ❖

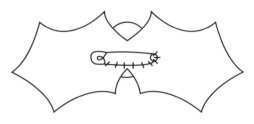

Fig. 6
Tack safety pin to back of pin.

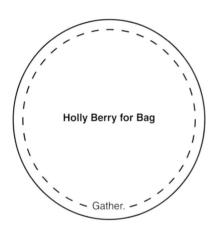

Holly Berry for Bag

Gather.

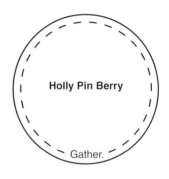

Holly Pin Berry

Gather.

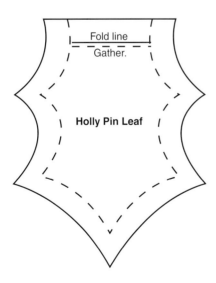

Fold line

Gather.

Holly Pin Leaf

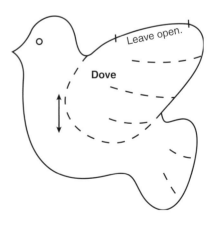

o

Leave open.

Dove

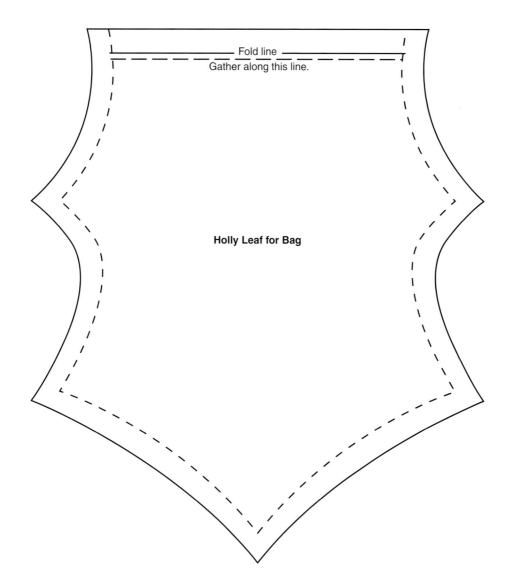

Fold line

Gather along this line.

Holly Leaf for Bag

Twinkle Toes Stockings

Put a little kick in new Christmas stockings to jazz up your merrymaking. Jester-style stockings made from rich fabrics and glamorous trims are easy to make and will be the talk of your holiday parties!

DESIGNS BY CAROL ZENTGRAF

Project Specifications
Stocking Size: 20 inches long

Materials
Velvet Stocking
- ⅔ yard embossed red velvet
- ⅔ yard coordinating plaid cotton for lining
- 34-inch-long red-and-white feather boa
- Green drapery tieback with 3- or 4-inch-long tassel
- 14 inches ¼-inch-wide ribbon for hanger
- Walking foot for your machine (optional)

Plaid Stocking
- ⅔ yard each 2 coordinating cotton plaids
- 34-inch-long red feather boa
- 1 yard red beaded trim
- ½ yard eyelash fringe trim
- Double-sided basting tape

Both Projects
- Pattern tracing cloth or paper
- Small amount of polyester fiberfill
- Permanent fabric adhesive
- All-purpose threads to match fabrics
- Basic sewing tools and equipment

Instructions
Velvet Stocking
Step 1. Enlarge the pattern on page 167 on pattern tracing cloth or paper and cut out. Note the cutting line for the rounded toe of the lining. Use the pattern to cut two stockings (reverse images) from the velvet and two from the lining fabric.

Step 2. With right sides together, sew the velvet stockings together along the side and lower edges using a ½-inch-wide seam. As you approach the curled-toe area, gradually decrease the seam width to ¼ inch, gradually returning to ½ inch to sew the remaining long edge (Fig. 1 on page 166) Turn right side out and lightly stuff the curled-toe area with fiberfill so it will keep its shape.

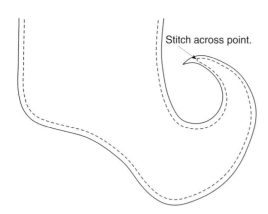

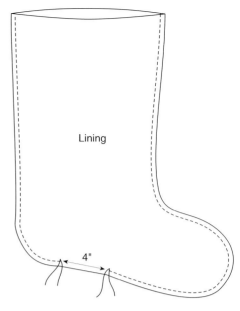

Fig. 1
Use ½" seams, narrowing to ¼" in the point.

Step 3. Sew the lining panels together, but leave a 4-inch-long opening in the center of the lower edge (Fig. 2).

Step 4. Place the velvet stocking inside the lining, aligning the upper edges and side seams; pin the upper edges together. Stitch ½ inch from the upper edges. To turn right side out, carefully pull the velvet stocking through the opening in the lining, turning the lining right side out. Turn the opening edges in on the lining and slipstitch together or edgestitch together by machine.

Step 5. Tuck the lining inside the stocking. Finger-press

Fig. 2
Leave 4" opening in lining.

the upper edge and side seams; do not iron. Topstitch ¼ inch from the upper edge to secure the lining.

Step 6. Fold the ribbon for the hanging loop in half and stitch through the center as shown in Fig. 3. Tuck the stitched end of the ribbon inside the stocking at the side seam and sew or glue in place.

Fig. 3
Stitch loop ends together.

Make It Yours

It's easy to emboss your own velvet with a rubber stamp when you use silk, rayon or rayon/acetate velvet. (Do not use nylon, polyester, cotton or any other washable velvet or velveteen). Select a thick rubber stamp with a wooden base and a large, bold motif. To emboss the velvet:

1. Place the stamp right side up on an ironing board. Place the velvet right side down over the stamp.

2. Lightly mist the wrong side of the velvet with water. Use a dry iron set on medium heat and firmly press the velvet on the stamp for 20 seconds. Avoid letting the steam holes touch the fabric and don't slide or move the iron while pressing. Lift the iron straight up. Allow the fabric to cool, and then remove from the stamp.

3. To care for embossed velvet, dry-clean without steam pressing when needed. Steam will remove embossed images.

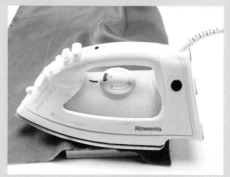

Step 7. Cut a 2-inch-long piece from the feather boa and glue in place around the end of the toe.

Step 8. Squeeze a line of fabric adhesive along the upper edge of the stocking front. Beginning at the side seam, finger-press the boa into the adhesive. Continue in the same manner to apply it to the upper edge of the back of the stocking. Wrap and glue the remainder of the boa around the stocking again, positioning it just below the first row.

Step 9. Position the tieback with the tassel at the center front of the stocking. Glue the cord in place at the side seams. Overlap and glue the cord ends to the stocking back.

Instructions
Plaid Stocking

Step 1. Enlarge the pattern on right on tracing paper or cloth and cut out. Cut two stockings from one plaid and two from the remaining plaid for the lining. Be sure to cut reverse images so you have a stocking front and back of each fabric.

Step 2. Follow Steps 2–6 for the velvet stocking to assemble the stocking and lining and sew them together.

Step 3. Apply basting tape to the back of the beaded trim header and the eyelash fringe header. Cut the beaded trim length in half. Working with one length at a time, remove the basting-tape backing and apply the trim around the stocking, placing it 1½ inches below the upper edge Apply the first length of trim and then add the second one on top of the first, offsetting the beads so they lie between the first row for a full look.

Step 4. Apply the eyelash fringe on top of the beaded trim header. Sew through all layers to secure.

Step 5. Apply the feather boa to the toe and the upper edge of the stocking as directed in Steps 7 and 8 for the velvet stocking. ❖

Make It Easy

Here is an easy way to separate embroidery floss to avoid tangling and knotting and ensure smooth stitching:

1. Cut the desired length of 6-strand embroidery floss.

2. With one end of the strands in your left hand between your thumb and index (pointing) finger, firmly grasp one strand of the floss with your right thumb and index finger (reverse the directions if you are left-handed).

3. Holding tight to the floss in your left hand, pull the single strand out of the group until it is free. Lay this on your lap or a table. Pull out two more strands in the same fashion and you have three untangled, untwisted strands of floss ready to be grouped for blanket stitching!

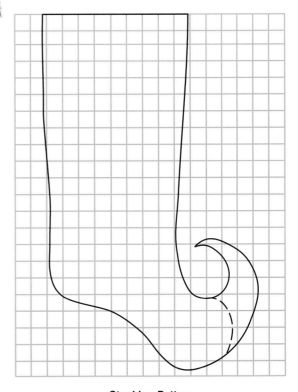

Stocking Pattern
1 square = 1"
Dashed line indicates
cutting line for lining pieces.

Wintry Pines

Use wool felt to create this table runner reminiscent of the penny rugs popularized during the Civil War era. It's the perfect table accent for the snowy days of winter.

DESIGN BY PAMELA J. CECIL

Project Specifications
Runner Size: 13 x 40 inches
Coaster Size: 4½ inches square

Materials
- 1¼ yards light tan felt
- ¼ yard green felt
- ¼ yard gold felt
- 9 x 12-inch piece (or scraps) brown felt
- 9 x 12-inch piece (or scraps) rust felt
- 4 skeins brown 6-strand embroidery floss
- 1 skein each green, rust and gold 6-strand embroidery floss
- Lightweight paper-backed fusible web
- Chenille/candlewicking needle
- All-purpose thread to match tan felt
- Press cloth
- Basic sewing tools

Instructions
Step 1. Cut two 15 x 36-inch pieces for the runner from the light tan felt.

Step 2. Trace the tab template on page 172 onto template plastic or poster board and cut out. Hold the tab pattern in place on a double layer of light tan felt and cut 12 double-layer tabs. Pin each pair of tabs together to keep them in matched pairs during the runner construction.

Step 3. Trace the appliqué templates on page 172 onto the paper side of the fusible web, leaving at least ¼ inch of space between motifs. Trace the required number of each one as directed on the templates.

Step 4. Cut out the shapes with a ⅛-inch-wide margin all around. Apply to felt of the appropriate color as given on the template. Cut out the shapes on the drawn lines and remove the paper backing from each one.

Step 5. Working on a large, flat surface, center a large rust felt "penny" on one of the tan felt rectangles. Center a gold penny on top of it. Referring to Fig. 1,

Fig. 1
Center Placement Diagram

arrange the stems, leaves, and hearts with gold pennies around the center circle. When satisfied with the arrangement, place a press cloth over the pieces and fuse in place following the manufacturer's directions.

Step 6. Referring to Fig. 2, position the lower end of a tree trunk 1 inch above each short end of the tan felt rectangle. Make sure the piece is centered from side to side and then fuse in place. Position the tree branches on each side of each trunk and a star above each one and fuse in place.

Fig. 2
Tree Placement Diagram

Step 7. Referring to Fig. 3, center a small gold penny on top of each remaining large rust penny. Place each stack on a pair of tabs about ½ inch from the lower edge. Fuse in place.

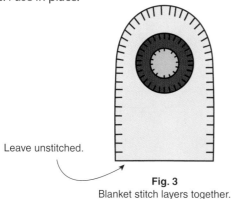

Leave unstitched.

Fig. 3
Blanket stitch layers together.

Step 8. Use 3 strands of embroidery floss for all stitching. To prevent tangles in your thread see Make It Easy on page 167. Blanket stitch around the applique edges using the following thread colors: brown for leaves and branches; green for tree trunks and stems; gold for hearts and large pennies; rust for stars and small pennies. **_Note:_** _When sewing the pennies in place on the tabs, set the lower tab of the pair aside while you stitch the pennies to the upper tab._ Then pin the lower tab to its mate to keep them together.
Brown: leaves and pine tree branches
Green: pine tree trunks and stems
Gold: hearts and large pennies
Rust: stars and small pennies

Step 9. Blanket stitch around the curved edges of the tabs using brown embroidery floss (Fig. 3).

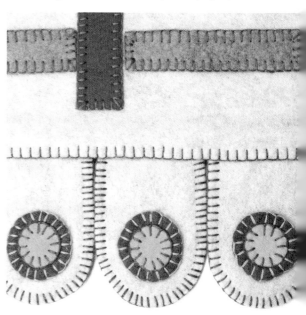

Step 10. Refer to Fig. 4 for Steps 10 and 11. With the appliquéd runner face up on a flat surface, arrange six tabs along each short end. Place them right sides together with raw edges even and stitched edges next to each other; pin in place. There should be a ¾-inch-wide allowance at each long edge. Machine baste the tabs in place.

Step 11. Pin the runner rectangles together with right sides facing. Stitch ¾ inch from the long raw edges and ¼ inch from the short ends. Leave a 5-inch-long opening in one long side for turning. Trim the seams to ¼ inch at the long edges. Turn the runner right side out and hand stitch the opening closed.

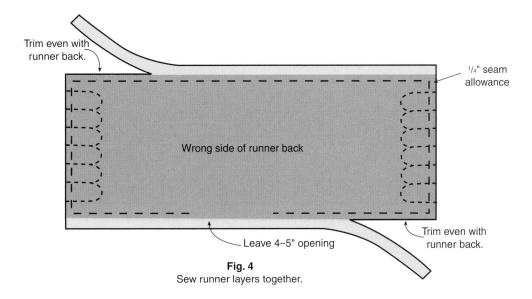

Fig. 4
Sew runner layers together.

Step 12. Using the brown floss, blanket stitch over all edges of the runner, stitching only over the edge of the top layer. Repeat on the back side of the rectangle.

Matching Coasters

1. Cut four double layers of tan felt, each measuring 2 inches square.

2. Using the runner appliqué templates, trace two hearts, two stars, 16 leaves, two stems and four pennies onto the paper side of the fusible web. Leave at least ¼ inch of space between the pieces. Cut out each shape with a ⅛-inch margin beyond the drawn lines.

3. Apply the fusible web to the appropriate-color felt for each piece (refer to the photos). Cut out on the traced lines and remove the paper backing.

4. Referring to the photos, position the appliqués on the top piece of each of the four pairs of tan felt and fuse in place following the manufacturer's directions. Use a press cloth to protect the felt.

5. Using 3 strands of embroidery floss, blanket stitch around the pieces using the following colors: brown for leaves; green for stems; gold for hearts; gold for the rust pennies; and rust for the gold pennies.

6. Use brown embroidery floss to blanket stitch the coaster layers together around all four edges. ❖

Why the Pennies?

Penny rugs are an old craft that has witnessed new popularity with quilters and sewers. The rugs originated in the United States around the time of the Civil War and were cut from worn woolen blankets, clothing and even soldiers' uniforms. Simplicity was the rule. Blanket-stitched shapes were sewn onto the tops of these first rugs. The term "penny rug" comes from tracing around coins on fabrics to create the small circular shapes. They were then cut and arranged in patterns on the rug tops and hand-stitched in place. They were also added to the border tabs that were sewn along the outer edges of the rugs. Traditionally, these rugs were used on tabletops, beds and chairs. Penny rugs today are also used as wall hangings, on mantels, and as decorative accents on sofa backs.

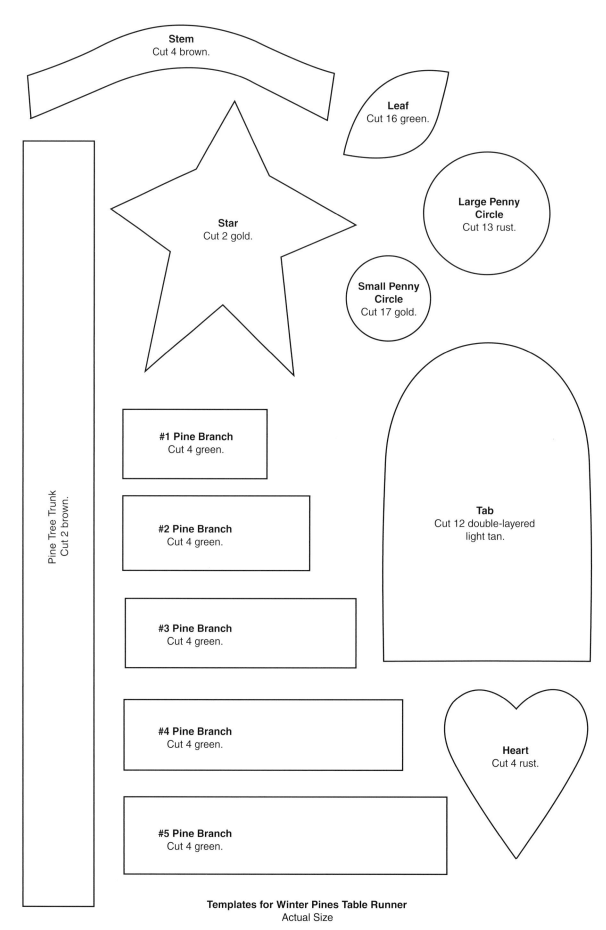

Stem
Cut 4 brown.

Leaf
Cut 16 green.

Star
Cut 2 gold.

Large Penny Circle
Cut 13 rust.

Small Penny Circle
Cut 17 gold.

Pine Tree Trunk
Cut 2 brown.

#1 Pine Branch
Cut 4 green.

#2 Pine Branch
Cut 4 green.

#3 Pine Branch
Cut 4 green.

Tab
Cut 12 double-layered
light tan.

#4 Pine Branch
Cut 4 green.

Heart
Cut 4 rust.

#5 Pine Branch
Cut 4 green.

Templates for Winter Pines Table Runner
Actual Size

Serger-Easy
Ornaments

It's easy to make a batch of decorative fabric ornaments like these. It's also a great way to practice and master turning smooth corners. Quilters' cottons with metallic accents are the perfect materials. Use as gifts or to decorate your own tree. Kids who are learning to use the serger will enjoy this project, too.

DESIGNS BY MARTA ALTO

Project Specifications

Gold: 5 x 5⅝ inches

Red/Green: 5 x 5⅝ inches

Red/Gold: 4½ x 5 inches

Green/Gold: 4 x 4¼ inches

Materials for One Ornament

1 (3 x 15-inch or 4 x 18-inch) strip of two contrasting fabrics

1 (3 x 1-inch or 4 x 18-inch) strip of paper-backed fusible web

- Decorative thread for the loopers—2 that blend or 2 of the same color. **Note:** *Try YLI Candlelight, Crown Pearl Rayon or Designer 6 or Madeira Decor 6.*
- All-purpose sewing thread to match color of decorative thread
- Rotary cutter, mat and ruler
- Serger
- Basic sewing tools and equipment
- Small beads for embellishment (optional)

Instructions

Step 1. Apply fusible web to the wrong side of one fabric strip following the manufacturer's directions.

Step 2. Remove the backing paper and fuse the strip to the wrong side of the remaining strip to make a double-layer fabric.

Step 3. Cut four 4-inch squares for the larger ornament or four 3-inch squares for the smaller ornament.

Step 4. Set up the serger with decorative thread on both loopers. Thread the right-hand needle with regular thread.

Step 5. Serge all four edges of each square, turning neat corners as you go (see the sidebar at bottom of page). *Do not trim the fabric as you serge.* Leave a ½-inch-long thread tail on each of three squares and a 3-inch-long tail on the fourth square.

Step 6. Stack the four squares with the same fabric facing up and tuck the ½-inch-long serger tails between the layers. Make a hanging loop with the 3-inch tail and tuck ½ inch of it into the layers with the other thread tails.

Step 7. Stitch diagonally from the loop to the opposite corner of the stacked squares backstitching at both ends. Be sure to catch the serger tails in the stitching.

Step 8. Bring the loose corners together, two at a time and pin. Also pin the layers together 2 inches from each point. Bartack the layers together by hand or machine at each pin using thread to match the color of the decorative serging.

Step 9. Add beads to the corners if desired. ❖

Cornering Practice

Turn a neat corner with your serger.

1. Serge over the raw edge right to the cut edge and one stitch past it. Raise the needle (Fig. 1).

2. *Note:* *Practice makes perfect on this step.* Carefully release the thread from the stitch finger. Use your finger to pull a little slack in the needle thread first to make this easier (Fig. 2). If you pull too much thread, simply pull the thread back up a bit—above the needle tension dial. On newer sergers, try gently pulling the fabric straight back to release the chain.

3. Pivot the fabric and lower the needle in the square at the upper edge of the corner. Continue serging to the next corner and repeat the process (Fig. 3).

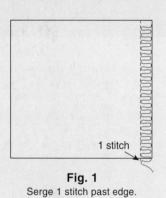

1 stitch

Fig. 1
Serge 1 stitch past edge.

1. Stack the squares, create the loop and stitch from the loop to the opposite corner.

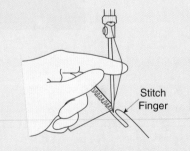

Stitch Finger

Fig. 2
Pivot square and use finger to pull a bit of slack in thread above needle point.

2. Bring loose corners together.

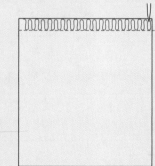

Fig. 3
Insert needle just inside upper edge.

3. Pin layers together 2 inches from each corner.

Fabric & Supplies

Page 8: *Flower Basket Bouquet*—Olfa-North America rotary-cutting tools, The Warm Company Warm & Natural batting, Pellon Consumer Products Wonder-Under fusible web, Coats & Clark sewing threads, Loew-Cornell Series 7550 1" wash brush, Delta Technical paints and matte varnish, Beacon Adhesives Glass, Metal & More and Hold the Foam! Glue, The Dow Chemical Company STYROFOAM brand foam, Offray Ribbon Company wire-edged ribbon, Prym-Dritz Fray Check seam sealant

Page 16: *Butterbees Bumbleflies Kitchen Ensemble*—The Warm Company Lite Steam-A-Seam 2, Insul-Bright needlepunched Insulated lining, Warm and Natural needled cotton batting

Page 24: *Stripe It Rich Pillow Duo*—Beacon Adhesives Fabri-Tac permanent fabric adhesive, Fairfield Processing Corp. Soft Touch pillow forms, The Warm Company Steam-A-Seam 2 fusible web tape, Waverly Fabrics #667512 Dunmore Stripe Sage

Page 31: *Spring Is Welcome Here*—The Warm Company Light Steam-A-Seam 2

Page 40: *Chenille Fancy Footstool*—Beacon Adhesives Fabri-Tac permanent fabric adhesive, Fabric Café Chenille

by the Inch, Cutting Guide and Chenille Brush, Fairfield Processing Corp. Soft Touch pillow form and Poly-fil Hi-loft batting

Page 50: *Sailing Through Summer*—June Tailor Quilter's Fusible Batting, Pellon Stitch and Tear stabilizer, Krylon metallic paint, Fiskars cutting tools, William E. Wright metallic rickrack, Aleene's Clear Gel Tacky Glue, Therm O Web HeatnBond Lite iron-on adhesive

Page 58: *Fat Quarter Confetti Jacket*—Timeless Treasures fabrics, The Warm Company Steam-A-Seam 2

Page 68: *Veggie Lover's Handbag*—Dover Clip-Art Series *Old-Fashioned Animal Cuts* and *Treasury of Animal Illustrations From Eighteenth Century Sources,* Therm O Web HeatnBond iron-on adhesive, Plaid Enterprises Picture This clear transfer medium, 3–M Scotchgard Fabric Protector, Welsh Products Inc. WPI Inkjet 2T Transfer Paper

Page 99: *Loop Tricks & Pick-Up Stix*—CPE wool and rayon felt

Page 102: *Quick-Change Pillow Toppers*—Beacon Adhesives Fabri-Tac permanent adhesive, Expo International eyelash fringe, Fairfield Processing Corp. Soft–Touch pillow form, Waverly #668720 Vineyard Scroll, #668690 Rutherford

Hill and #668680 Canyon Road fabrics (color Merlot) from the Sonoma Valley Collection

Page 106: *Something to Crow About Penny Rug*—Cleo And Me wool felt, Therm O Web HeatnBond Lite iron-on adhesive

Page 111: *Juice-Can Jazz Footstool*—Beacon Adhesives Fabri-Tac permanent fabric adhesive, The Gorilla Glue Company Gorilla Glue, Waverly fabrics

Page 114: *Leaf Peeper's Jacket*—Weeks Dye Works™ hand over-dyed wool

Page 118: *Falling Leaves Lap Quilt*—Airtex Roll-and-Quilt Cotton Blend Batting, Borders Made Easy, quilting pattern #111

Page 123: *A Fall Welcome*—The Warm Company Lite Steam-A-Seam 2

Page 128: *Sassy Sunflowers*—Therm O Web HeatnBond Lite iron-on adhesive

Page 134: *Tabletop Elegance*—Beacon Adhesives Fabri-Tac permanent adhesive, Expo International tassel trim #IR2567BB

Page 138: *Let it Snow!*—Fabric Café Chenille By The Inch, cutting guide and chenille brush, Just Another

Button Company polymer clay buttons, The Warm Company Steam-A-Seam 2 fusible web

Page 149: *Think Snow*—Therm O Web HeatnBond Lite fusible web, Pellon Stitch-n-Tear stabilizer, Krylon Premium Metallic paint, Wm. E. Wright metallic cord, Kreinik Fine (#8) Braid #001 Silver, Fiskars cutting tools, June Tailor Quilter's Fusible Batting, Sulky Holo Shimmer #145-6001, Aleene's Clear Gel Tacky Glue and Jewel-It glues, Tulip Silver Permanent Fabric Glitter Spray

Page 156: *Crazy for Quilting*—Dritz Wonder Tape double-sided basting tape, Fairfield Processing Corp. Poly-fil polyester fiberfill

Page 159: *Organza Surprises*—Unique's rubber/vinyl-coated loop turner

Page 164: *Twinkle Toes Stockings*—Beacon Adhesives Fabri-Tac permanent adhesive, Prym-Dritz Wonder Tape double-sided, self-adhesive basting tape, Expo International beaded trim #IR2688PL and eyelash fringe #IR17854GR

Page 168: *Wintry Pines*—Wool felt from The Quilter's Husband Rainbow Classic Felts and Cleo and Me, Therm O Web HeatnBond Lite iron-on adhesive

Sewing Services

The following companies provided fabric and/or supplies for projects in this book. If you are unable to locate a product locally, contact the manufacturers listed below for the closest retail or mail-order source in your area.

ASHRO
(800) 274-7476
www.easternartarcade.com

Beacon Adhesives
(914) 699-3400
www.beacon1.com

Conso Products
(800) 845-2431
www.cosno.com

David Textiles
(800) 548-1818

Dritz
www.dritz.com

Thai Silks
(800) 722-7455
www.thaisilks.com

Expo International
(800) 542-4367
www.expointl.com

Fairfield Processing
(800) 980-8000
www.ply-fil.com

Fiskars
(800) 950-0203
www.fiskars.com

Flights of Fancy
(800) 530-8745
www.flightsoffancyboutique.com

**Hollywood Trims/
Prym-Dritz Corp.**
www.dritz.com

Husqvarna Viking
(800) 358-0001
www.husqvarnaviking.com

Jackman's Fabrics
(800) 758-3742
www.jackmanfabrics.com

Kwik Sew Pattern Co.
(612) 521-7651
www.Kwiksew.com

Logantex Inc.
(800) 223-2004

MacPhee Workshop
(888) 622-7233
www.macpheeworkshop.com

Melissa Becker Designs
(800) 356-0020
www.melissabeckerdesigns.com

Mokuba
(212) 869-8900

**Purrfection Artistic
Wearables**
(800) 691-4293
www.purrfection.com

Sulky of America
(800) 874-4115
www.sulky.com

Tandy Leather Company
(888) 890-1611
www.tandyleather.com

The Beadery
(401) 539-2432
www.thebeadery.com

Leather Factory
(713) 880-8235
www.leatherfactory.com

The Sewing Workshop
(800) 466-1599
www.sewingworkshop.com

The Warm Company
(800) 234-9276
www.warmcompany.com

Therm O Web
(800) 323-0799
www.thermoweb.com

TorayUltrasuede
(732) 431-1550
www.torayusa.com/tua

YLI Corporation
(800) 296-8139
www.ylicorp.com

Special Thanks

We would like to thank the talented sewing designers whose work is featured in this collection

Marta Alto
Serger-Easy Ornaments, 173

Pam Archer
Green Thumb Gardening Apron, 81
Place Mats With Pizzazz, 27
Silken Eye-Catchers, 64

Mary Ayres
Leaf-Peeper's Jacket, 114

Pamela J. Cecil
Something to Crow About
Penny Rug, 106
Wintry Pines, 168

Denise Clason
Flower Basket Bouquet, 8

Karen Dillon
Loop Tricks & Pick-Up Stix, 99

Nancy Fiedler
Pajama Party, 55

Lucy Gray
Dance With Me Evening Bag, 153
Easter Bonnet Handbag, 35
Felted Fancy Sweater Bag, 94
Veggie Lover's Handbag, 68

Annabelle Keller
Sailing Through Summer, 50
Think Snow, 149

Pamela Lindquist
Butterbees & Bumbleflies
Kitchen Ensemble, 16
Falling Leaves Lap Quilt, 118
Hearts-All-Around Neckroll, 44

Judith Sandstrom
Sassy Sunflowers, 128

Jane Schenck
Shell Seekers Porch Set, 74

Diana Stunnel-Dunsmore
Organza Surprises, 159

Meg Tryba
Kissy Fish Lap Quilt, 85

Julie Weaver
A Fall Welcome, 123
Spring Is Welcome Here, 31

Barbara Weiland
Fat Quarter Confetti Jacket, 58

Eileen Westfall
Christmas in the Neighborhood, 1
Go Fly a Kite Wall Quilt, 12

Hope Yoder
Splish-Splash Swim Cover-Up, 90

Carol Zentgraf
Chenille Fancy Footstool, 40
Crazy for Quilting, 156
Juice-Can Jazz Footstool, 111
Let It Snow!, 138
Quick-Change Pillow Toppers, 102
Stripe It Rich Pillow Duo, 24
Tabletop Elegance, 134
Twinkle Toes Stockings, 164